DEDICATION

This book is dedicated to my parents Earl & Lola Trent Sr. who raised me to serve the Lord with all my heart, mind and soul;
To my loving wife, Janice and daughters Noelle, Andrea and Jessica who are my richest blessings and greatest gifts,
And to the future generations of God's sun-kissed children.

To Mr Samuel McKinney
May God Bless you
abundantly

Rev Earl Trent Jr

CONTENTS

A CHALLENGE TO THE BLACK CHURCH

by

Rev. Earl D. Trent, Jr., D. Min.

African American Images
CHICAGO

Front cover design by Harold Carr

Copyright © 2004 by Rev. Earl D. Trent Jr., D. Min.

First edition, first printing

Printed in the United States of America

ISBN: 0-974900-01-X

ACKNOWLEDGEMENTS

I am very grateful to the many persons who helped to make this work possible. I am especially indebted to Ms. Sherri Washington who did most of the typing of the initial manuscript and managed to decipher most of my handwritten notations. I thank Dr. Cain Hope Felder, and Dr. Willard Ashley for their review and comments early on that encouraged and helped to shape the direction of my thoughts. I must acknowledge my doctoral mentors, Dr. Jeremiah A. Wright, Jr. and Dr. Jawanza Kunjufu for their influence and development of my Afrocentric perspective. I am also indebted to Dr. Claud Anderson for his probing questions about the plight of Black people served as catalyst for this book. Most of all I am grateful for the people of the Florida Avenue Baptist Church, especially the Wednesday night bible study, whose questions and prayers proved invaluable assets.

PREFACE

Nearly everyone has an opinion about the Black Church its role, its shortcomings, its present state, and what it should be doing for the future of the Black community. Far too many of these opinions are from the outside looking in, or based on a childhood remembrance or a very cursory knowledge of the church. This is a collection of essays written **to** the Black Church, not **about** it. It is a collection of essays grounded in personal knowledge of the Black Church from childhood through adolescence. It is a testimony of my experience as one who looked for a time from the outside, rejoined, became active as a lay person, and for the last twenty years served as a pastor.

There is no personal axe to grind against the church, but rather out of respect and profound love of the Lord and the Black Church and its mission, I submit these essays to you. They are challenging, but that challenge comes out of a firm belief in Jesus' mandate that the church must be the "light of the world and salt of the earth" and take seriously the plight and crisis of Black people in the 21st century. It is not my challenge, but the challenge and call of the Gospel.

You will note that these essays are written in the first person. This collection of essays is for Black Christians. It is not "anti" anyone. I am simply describing the intended audience. Most writings about Black life are apologetic to the non-Black audience, explaining us to them and to ourselves. These essays are written to Black people. Therefore I have chosen to write in the first person.

This is an open invitation for candor. Though at times these essays seem somewhat sermonesque, they are not really sermons and never have been delivered as sermons, though their content has been part of many sermons. Their intent is to engage us in a different type of dialogue, one that involves criticism without pretense or the rose–colored religious language that is often used when we talk about the church. Yet this critique is not without love and practical solutions, which I hope will spark further discussion among us.

First and foremost let me state my foundational premise: We as a Black Church must form for ourselves a viable, practical Black theology that informs our response to contemporary situations as a people. In their seminal work *Black Theology: a Documentary History* Gayraud Wilmore and James Cone date the beginning of Black theology to around 1966[1]. Wilmore notes that "Black people have done theology out of their guts, out of the individual and collective experiences of struggle." This is not unlike the message of the Bible, Wilmore asserts, for its message did not come out of the monasteries, libraries, and debates among philosophers and kings. When the Black theology movement entered the world of the academy in the late 1960s, it was only then that the wails and moans of Black people were institutionalized and articulated from a relevant, culturally appropriate Christian perspective.

Cone and Wilmore trace the changes in Black theology up to the 1980s, but by and large their history is a dialogue among the upper ranks of clergy and scholars. There has been some acceptance of Black theology and Black consciousness by the Black Church, as evidenced by new stained glass windows with Black images, Kente cloth choir and clergy robes, and Kwanzaa celebrations, along with Christmas and wedding ceremonies altered to include "jumping the broom."

In the most important areas of worship and biblical interpretation, Black theology has not taken hold. There is a lack of a preached theology that thoroughly includes Black theological expression on any consistent basis. This is the norm throughout the traditional Black and White denominations, the Full Gospel movement, the Pentecostals movement, and especially the TV ministries.

For example, in the spring, 2004, issue of *The African American Pulpit,* there are 18 sermons written by bishops of various denominations and assemblies. Only one mentions the plight of Black people specifically and the problems that are particular to Black people. (Bishop Linda Lee, my classmate from United Theological Seminary, 1994 Doctor of Ministry class in Afrocentric pastoring and preaching). These are bishops who influence and oversee other Black ministers, and their sermons are presented as models for the modern pulpit. These sermons, though well crafted, are stunning indicators of the vacuum that exists between Black theology in the academic world and Black theology in practice. This is not to be taken lightly. The words of exhortation in Ephesians 4: 14, *We must no longer be children, tossed to and fro by every wind of doctrine, by people's trickery, by their craftiness in deceitful scheming...,* are reminders that the goal is a mature Christian faith that is not faddish but well-integrated between thought and practice. Unless we accomplish that, we are subject to the whims of the religious marketplace and the schemes and tricks of those who do not have our best interests in mind.

These essays are to challenge both clergy and laity to assess where we are as a people, as a church, and as a community. Each of these essays is based upon an Afrocentric reinterpretation of some of the Biblical texts that have been most important to the Black Church. By making our history as Black people the foundation of our encounter with God, we gain new insight into and meaning from the scriptures. Secondly, we are forced to evaluate our purpose, mission, and contemporary situation as God's people.

The first group of essays is focused on the basic assumptions we make about our faith as Black people and examines whether these assumptions are in keeping with the biblical texts. The second group of essays is a direct challenge to some of the inappropriate behaviors we perpetuate or allow to exist in our churches and communities. These essays question the relevancy of our popular theology to the contemporary age. The final group of essays probes the future direction of the Black Church, as we live our faith as the people of God in the 21st century.

As an introduction to each section, I quote a verse of an old hymn, *A Charge to Keep*. It is not often sung now, but it is a foundation of our history as Black Church people. It is a reminder that our Christian walk is much larger than our individual selves and our individual desires. The song originates in God's call to us and has roots in His saving acts in our particular story as a people. Therefore, we have large responsibilities and a sacred accountability that engages all the facets of our lives.

As the writer of the prison epistle in Ephesians pleads, we must walk worthy of the vocation to which we are called. It would do us good to hear that old hymn again. We need to hear it again and listen for the beat underneath the rhythm and the history that still lives and waits to engage our minds, bodies, and souls.

INTRODUCTION

I cannot remember the first time I heard the song *A Charge to Keep*. I simply remember growing up, muttering to myself that it was a lousy tune. There was nothing to tap your foot to, and that was important to a youngster. (We did not clap our hands in those days.) It did not seem to go anywhere musically. Mercifully, it was a short hymn, but not without penalty. One had to make that full octave jump in the third measure. This quickly became the place to brace yourself. Some of the sainted mothers of the church who nurtured us with firm pinches and withering looks that froze you on the side of good when mischief called you to another path, seemed to attack this note with sacred zeal. Occasionally they hit it, most often they brought to life the 100th Psalm: *make a joyful noise to the Lord.*

Still it was a haunting tune. Something about that song got underneath you and locked onto your soul. It was a somber, sobering statement. The plainness of the tune punched up the power of the words. It was an uncomfortable song. There was heaviness to it—not the weightiness of carrying something dead and broken, but the heaviness of something alive and awful. At the time I did not know what, but something was going on deep, deep within.

I do remember when that something coalesced and a new consciousness was born. It was in my aunt's church in

Virginia during a devotional before Communion. A senior deacon stood up. He fixed his aged eyes on some past event that we could not see but was still vivid to him. In a raspy baritone voice, half singing, almost speaking, he sang "A charge to keep I have." In that same half singing, almost speaking tone the congregation recited the phrase.

The deacon moved to the next phrase. The congregation followed him. They did all four verses that way. It was long meter singing. It was the remnants of a time that even then was beginning to collect the cobwebs of the forgotten. What got to me was the sound—a long, slow mournful sound, an awful sound that filled the space between the cushionless pews and the wooden rafters. No piano, no organ, just Black voices: high yellow, coal, caramel, mud brown, Georgia red, colored folk, Negro—Black voices. Those voices got underneath that song and stretched it.

They stretched that song like they themselves had been stretched by life. No, like they had been racked by life. They had been tortured with malice aforethought until their divine image of self broke in the red Virginia clay, and red dust mixed with dark–running blood. Like a carcass repeatedly run over on the highway, their hopes and dreams lay on life's road. That Sunday I heard that hymn stretched until its underneath became its top and its haunting call was no longer hidden. Something like a deep seismic wave rolled through that little church and shook my soul until my teeth rattled. Then I understood the haunting nature of that song.

It was the work song of nameless backs and hands straining on a thick rope trying to drag forward something huge. It is not an individual declaration but a recognition that each person has to pull their weight, for we are all involved in something much larger than ourself. It is our soul self. We have a charge to keep. A charge given by those whose lives lay unfulfilled, cut short, ground down, and shattered along a million miles of history. Their voices give bottom to that wave and are the core of that seismic tide. No words, no explanation, no plea, just a moan of long pain and the grunt of longer labor.

A charge to keep I have

A God to glorify

Who gave his Son my soul to save,

And fit it for the sky[2]

IS THERE A BALM IN GILEAD?

The harvest is past, the summer is ended,
and we are not saved.
For the hurt of my poor people I am hurt,
I mourn, and dismay has taken hold of me.
Is there no balm in Gilead?
Is there no physician there?
Why then has the health of my poor people
not been restored?

Jeremiah 8: 20-22 NRSV

Moments of self-revelation are strange. They are not magical—mysterious, but not magical. When that stuff we placed on the back burner of the subconscious moves to the front of our consciousness, it seems magical, but it is not. If it were magic, these moments could be conjured by incantation or summoned by some psychic, but they cannot. They simply, unpredictably, happen. If we label these strange moments miraculous, we would have a more accurate description. When our inarticulate emotions find voice, or when the inevitable event suddenly arrives, it is in that moment that we are given an opportunity for a closer, deeper encounter with God. That is a wondrous miracle.

I was in a hotel in 1995 while attending a convention when my hair turned gray. I woke up early, turned on the bathroom light, peered in the mirror, and my hair was gray.

People had mentioned it before. My wife and children had teased me before about strands inhabiting the forest. Friends, particularly those I did not see often, would make remarks, but that moment staring into the bathroom mirror, the epiphany took place. I was gray. The no–longer–deniable fact fully hit. Why then? Why at that moment? I do not know. I had looked in mirrors before, plenty of them. If I had known that this particular mirror would be the accessory to the moment, I would have never checked into that room. I would have been perfectly content to continue living in my private definition of reality. "It's just a few flecks, it's just the light." I turned gray that morning, and that reality was not going to be denied any more except by outright lying.

Those moments of self-revelation, in their unpredictability and uncontrollable nature, push chaos into our lives. What is most troubling in those moments are the elements of self-evaluation that come along with the package. I realized that turning gray meant I was older. That prompted some uncomfortable questions: "What have I done on my way to this moment?" What will I do now? What will I do differently?

You will do things differently after a moment of revelation. It is impossible not to do so and remain sane. Revelation demands evaluation, and evaluation is to be avoided at all cost for it inevitably leads to change. Change is demanding and discomforting for most of us. So individually and collectively we go to great lengths to place ourselves outside the parameters of evaluation, particularly

Is There a Balm in Gilead?

self-evaluation for it can be the most difficult. There is no one to blame or hide behind. We want to avoid it personally and collectively, but revelation and its cousin, evaluation, will track us down.

Unknowingly, that morning when I turned gray, I had stumbled into the world of Jeremiah, the sixth–century B.C. prophet from the village of Anathoth. He too knew of the mysterious dimension of denial and self-revelation. He also knew of the inevitable subconscious working its way from delay to ultimate priority in a flash of insight. Is there a balm in Gilead?

These words that gave rise to the Negro spiritual have generally been read as a question to be answered. Our ancestors answered affirmatively in song, but for the prophet Jeremiah, it was his moment in the mirror. It was that unpredictable moment when he came face to face with the reality of the state of his people and the reality of his own state of being. Only God knew how long he had been trying to avoid that moment. What private definitions of reality he had conjured to delay the inevitable, we will never know. What inflated public arguments had been offered to mitigate the telling signs of societal decay are not recorded. The private mutterings of street–corner commentators about the lack of strong leaders and lost role models of a nonexistent era were ignored in his day as in ours.

Perhaps this moment was triggered by Jeremiah reflecting upon the unspeakable kernel of truth in the disparaging stereotypes of his people's communal inabilities and

3

failings. We do not know. We do know that some time after the early harvest of summer and the later harvest of fall it hit the prophet of Anathoth. The moment of revelation tracked him down and pounced on him with the full weight of its horror. "The harvest is past, the summer is ended, and we are not saved."

Why this revelation of doom at this particular moment, is a question for speculation, but the elements of evaluation are clear. Chaos was thrown into the mix of their daily lives. There was something grievously wrong in that North African nation of Israel (The term Middle East was not used until 1945). Things were not well with this chosen people. The fabric of their society, that which makes a people a nation and a community, was ripping at the seams.

Deeply troubling events had been unfolding for some time, but now the putrid smell of death was in the air and there was no more denying. There was something frightfully askew in Israel. The incense of prayers could not cover it. Despite their knowledge of the Law and the writings of earlier prophets, the foundation of their faith was shaky. You can almost hear the tremor in his voice as Jeremiah dares to face what he had expected to come, hoped would not, but now had arrived.

It is difficult to come face to face with one's personal fears, but it is shear terror to see the pillars of an entire people's philosophy and faith shaken. The momentous size of such an event can push one to the brink of insanity. Because a mere prosaic statement will not convey the scope

Is There a Balm in Gilead?

and magnitude of this revelation, Jeremiah uses poetic form and a rhetorical question to express what he has discovered. "Is there no balm in Gilead? Is there no physician there?" Of course there is still medicine in the town known for its healing ointments. Of course there are still doctors performing services. What is now obvious to the prophet is that the people, his people, are still sick. The medicine has been applied, but his people are still sick. Medical services have been performed, but his people are still sick. Isolated illnesses have become contagious, and an epidemic or perhaps even a pandemic threatens. The entire nation is in trouble. There is no denying it except by outright lying, for the unpredictable moment of epiphany has caught Jeremiah.

The Israelites' understanding of themselves as God's chosen people who will never be removed from their land (based on God's promise made to the patriarch Abraham) no longer fits the reality of their circumstances. Their chosen status will no longer protect or preserve their homeland despite their prayers, worship, and laws. Disaster is coming. Jeremiah did not want to see it or proclaim it, but it is of no avail. He has been caught in the undeniable moment in the mirror. So he proclaims and weeps for his people.

If Black America stares in the mirror, we will realize that the images do not match the proclamations of our civil rights leaders, politicians, business persons, and preachers. They proclaim that Black America has made

5

progress, though it still has "a ways to go." The reality is that we, Black America, as diverse as we may be, are in crisis. We have made progress, but so has everyone else— and mostly at our expense.

This public progress response often points to a rising number of middleclass Blacks and the number of elected Black officials as evidence of our progress. Those of us who have been in the once forbidden boardrooms and have been allowed to rub shoulders as quasi-contemporaries with the ruling class of this country have seen what the top looks like in lifestyle, wealth, and power. Though it's largely un-spoken, we super-privileged Blacks know that substantial progress, especially for the mass of Black people, is a myth. While some are no longer scraping bottom, the top has moved much, much farther away.

Black America has arrived at a critical moment in history. We have arrived at a point of self-revelation and evaluation. It is time we stare in the mirror and look at the private definition of reality that no longer fits our circumstance. It is time to move beyond the song *There Is a Balm in Gilead* and wrestle with the indictment in the actual text:

> *The harvest is past, the summer is ended, and we are not saved.... Is there no Balm in Gilead? Is there no physician there? Why then has the health of my poor people not been restored?*
>
> Jeremiah 8: 22

Is There a Balm in Gilead?

Claud Anderson in his book *PowerNomics* cites a statistic that helps to put our economic "achievements" in perspective. On the eve of the Civil War when almost 100 percent of Black America was in slavery, the total estimated aggregate wealth that Black people had acquired was ½ of 1 percent of the wealth of this country. Presently, 100 percent of Black people are free and the aggregate wealth of Black America is still only ½ of 1 percent of the total wealth of this country.[3] We have not moved. When confronted with facts like this, too many of us as Black Christians usually are quick to respond piously that money is the root of all evil. The actual text states that *love* of money is the root of all evil (I Timothy 6: 10a). Let us confront the uncomfortable, for in our world, money is a necessity.

Poetically, Jeremiah probes the conscience of his people and reveals that something is not working. It is imperative that they, as God's chosen people, recognize that something has gone awry. Jeremiah appeals not to the king and the government, but to what has most influence on his people, their religion. In a similar manner, we turn to the Black Church.

We in the Black Church must first take a look in the mirror and see what stares back for a number of reasons. First of all, it is our mandate and mission to care for our community. We are commissioned to be the light and the salt, the preserving agent, of the world of our people. The Black Church has a vital role in promoting a high code of conduct and ending the inappropriate behavior that shackles our minds. Too often sexual behaviors, abuse, and sexual harassment in both pulpit and pew are ignored or labeled as "indiscretions" and never seriously addressed. We further fail to urge and model fiscal responsibility for the dollars that pass through our hands, and we fail to actively support our own people in business.

Secondly, the Black Church is virtually the only institution that is solely controlled by Black folk (although in some areas that is no longer true). Liberation is about ownership and control.

Third, the Black Church is most fluid as an institution in our own interclass structure. It is the only place where the strength of class division loses some of its detrimental impact. I emphasize *some*. Unfortunately, class and color divisions still have a great deal of unspoken influence in our lives.

What will we see as the Black Church when we look in the mirror? Black Americans go to church at a higher percentage rate than any other group in America. Our preachers preach better. Our services are livelier and longer. We give a higher percentage of our income to the church, more than any other group in America. We are represented in all the major denominations and have led the Pentecostal and now the Full Gospel movement, yet we lead the nation in five major negative categories: More crime, more unemployment, more disease and bad health, more AIDS, and more STD (sexually transmitted disease) exist in our

Is There a Balm in Gilead?

neighborhoods than in other neighborhoods of America.

Nearly 40 percent of Black America is below or near the national poverty line. What is wrong with this picture? The grim haunting truth is that "the harvest is past, the summer is ended," and we are not doing very well. These are harsh words and a harsh evaluation. But before you stop reading, first figure out who is to blame. If the God we serve is just, why are we at the bottom heap of society as a people? Though we worship and pray loud and long, the undeniable fact is that we as a people are losing ground. Is there something wrong with God?

There are those who would be quick to answer yes. Convert to another religion is their solution. Yet the roots of our sojourn in this country are Christian roots. We as a people have survived the most harrowing journey of any people on earth through our faith. Our progress has been marked by a strong belief in calling on Jesus. Has the God who brought us through historically become incapable? I say emphatically no! Just as Jeremiah was questioning the plight of his people and concluded that not the medicine or lack of balm, but something else was wrong. By raising the question publicly, he was forcing Israel to recognize that something was deeply wrong. As always, before any solution can be proposed or prayed about, we must first realize that something is wrong. We have a problem!

Acknowledging that we ourselves are a good deal of the problem is difficult. To continue in the same manner of preaching and teaching on traditional and the latest fad themes and simply continuing to do "what we always have done" is a highly questionable course of action. It does not mean we have lost our faith, but we must face the reality that what we are doing can be out of step with the needs of our people and out of step with the will of God.

We might be asking the Lord for the wrong things, just as the Israelites did in Jeremiah's day. They no more wanted to hear that they, the chosen people, were doing something wrong than we, God's new chosen people, want to acknowledge the depth of our problem. The core of our dilemma revolves around an incomplete interpretation of the Good News message.

AN AWESOME DECLARATION

The Spirit of the Lord is upon me,
Because he has anointed me to bring good
news to the poor,
He has sent me to proclaim release to the
captives
And recovery of sight to the blind,
To let the oppressed go free,
To proclaim the year of the Lord's favor.

Luke 4: 18-19

The Gospel, or the Good News, is given in four perspectives, those of Matthew, Mark, Luke, and John. This might seem to be a firm grasp of the obvious, however, sometimes that which is right before our eyes is not clearly recognizable. Of those four perspectives, three are similar and one is quite different. Each of these perspectives has a different emphasis, yet all of them are the Gospel.

What is the point? There are actually two. One is that there can be a difference in what is emphasized without negating another viewpoint as long as there is a common objective. Secondly, we have some choice as to which part of the Gospel message we emphasize. That choice should not be based solely on personal whim but on God's leadership as revealed in the events and situations of the world in which we find ourselves. A good illustration is from our own history. Alice Sewell remembers the religious message during slavery:

> Dey did 'low us to go to church on Sunday about two miles down de public road, and dey hired a white preacher to preach to us. He never did tell us nothing but be good servants, pick up old marse and old misses' things about de place, and don't steal no chickens or pigs and don't lie about nothing. Den dey baptize you and call dat, you got religion. Never did say nothing 'bout a slave dying and going to heaven. When we die, dey bury us next day and you is just like any of de cattle dying on de place. We used to slip off in de woods in de old slave days on Sunday evening way down in de swamps to sing and pray to our own liking. We pray for dis day of freedom.[4]

Clearly the master's religious message was based solely on his self-interest, as was the slave's. But the slave's focus was the noble quest for freedom; the slave master's was simply greed. The serious but seldom asked question now is, What do we as Black folk emphasize in the Gospel and why?

It is safe to say that the emphasis in most Black churches is the condition of our souls. Mostly, we emphasize

An Awesome Declaration

salvation up front and personal. From the pulpit we ask, "Do you have a right relationship with God?" or more colloquially, "Do you know Jesus?" This relationship is highly personal and places the emphasis on loving one another, forgiveness, and the manifestation of the Holy Spirit in worship and song. Often this emphasis involves little social context or communal responsibility.

Why do we focus on the deeply personal? This emphasis has two sources. One is from slavery, where there was an emphasis on personal salvation and heavenly reward. Many slaves found it difficult to believe that they could receive reward during their lifetime. Therefore, they prayed to at least get into heaven.

The second source is the Protestant evangelical movement. The emphasis on personal salvation has inundated the airwaves, as control of most religious programming rests in the hands of this evangelical movement. There is very little mainline denominational religious programming except in local pockets and almost no Afrocentric Christian religious programming. The evangelical emphasis is a curious mixture of personal salvation and the American mythology of rugged individualism and the self-made man.

If there are aspects of our lives that are not going well, the first diagnostic question from the evangelical perspective is, "What is wrong with me?" The individual's relationship with God is diagnosed as "off kilter." The believer thinks that he must be operating outside the will of God or his life would be more "successful." Through the

13

power of well-produced, slick media, this message has been promoted, and we as Black Christians have, by and large, accepted it without substantive criticism.

It is imperative and helpful to look at what Jesus emphasized and how he understood his mission. The Gospel of Luke records the first sermon of Jesus in his own hometown of Nazareth. We begin with the text that Jesus read.

> *The Spirit of the Lord is upon me,*
> *Because he has anointed me to bring good news*
> *to the poor,*
> *He has sent me to proclaim release to the*
> *captives*
> *And recovery of sight to the blind,*
> *To let the oppressed go free,*
> *To proclaim the year of the Lord's favor.*
>
> Luke 4: 18-19

Isaiah 61 was a very well–known text, similar to Paul's chapter on love, as well as Psalms 23, 27, and 100. He read only part of the chapter, but the rest was generally known by the congregation and the initial readers of Luke's Gospel. Isaiah 61 was generally known as the chapter of promise, hope, and liberation. It was not simply a promise that God would bless them abundantly; it was seen as the fulfillment of the Jubilee promise of Leviticus 25. In that promise all debts are cancelled and the land reverts to its original owners. Isaiah 61 gave Israel hope, for it promised that their nation, which had long been occupied, would

An Awesome Declaration

no longer be the doormat of the world. There was a crisis in leadership, and the people had been looking for a new king, an earthly Messiah. The full text announced not only the Messiah but also the dawning of a new age.

In other words, this text did not exist in a cultural vacuum. Jesus chose to read it because it addressed the needs of the people in that time, place, and circumstance. It is also viable for us, but only insofar as we note the time, place, and circumstances of our situation does this Word become relevant, in other words, a living Word.

We must take care to avoid a premature interpretation of the text even as we initially read it. Many tend to read the text "The Spirit of the Lord is upon me because He has anointed me". But when we spiritualize this text and misdirect its emphasis, it becomes abstract and powerless, as if some vaporous anointing drifted mysteriously down from heaven and gave Jesus a glowing presence. That is the indicator that He is sent by God. Jesus has *the anointing.* This might satisfy our Disneyland fantasy, but it is not the emphasis of the text.

What the text emphasizes is a causative declaration. "The Spirit of the Lord is upon me because He has anointed me to bring Good News to the poor" is the complete thought. Because I bring Good News to the poor, I can declare that the Spirit of the Lord is upon me. That is a much more concrete, relevant, and powerful statement, especially if we understand who the poor are. The poor are a specific group. It is not a spiritual label such as "the poor in spirit." No, "the poor" is a specific economic class.

Though integral to the functioning of society, the poor were overlooked by society. Our ancestors fit squarely in this group. Black slaves in America could be labeled three–fifths of a human being for congressional count, sold as property, inherited, whipped, killed, and thrown into un-marked graves because they were overlooked by society and denied the fruits of the society they labored to create. These slaves were an integral part of the economy. They provided the labor needed so others could live well. In many instances slaves outnumbered Whites, but they were mere property, not persons. The door of societal benefits was shut against them.

In the first century, this group, the poor, consisted of slaves, semi-slaves, servants, the disabled, and the peas-ants. These marginal groups received little notice and few benefits from the society in which they lived. The good news is that though forgotten by society, they were not for-gotten by God. Though shut out of society, they were not shut out by God. This is in fact the litmus test and the causative part of the declaration. I know that the Spirit of the Lord is upon me because He has anointed me to bring Good News to those who are usually overlooked. Truly, only a God whose benevolence is far different from that of human beings would be concerned about the poor.

However, that is only part of the Good News. Again, there is a tendency to over–spiritualize. The great news is that the poor will not suffer poverty any longer.

An Awesome Declaration

Jesus ends the reading where the text makes a declaration that it is the acceptable year of the Lord, the year of Jubilation. This year of Jubilation was an economic rearrangement. It was a leveling of the practical economic playing field. It is the ultimate statement of faith for it directly affects the economic order. Money and wealth are the last things we allow God to rule over. Our spirituality by and large, ceases to exist in these areas. Yet they are the first areas Jesus addresses.

I have good news for the poor. All debts are canceled. You now have a chance to start over. You now will receive benefits for your labor and be able to partake of the fruits of society. Your God sees, knows, and has not forgotten. It is the acceptable year of the Lord.

Why have we ignored this economic emphasis of the Gospel? Is it less spiritual? Clearly Jesus did not think so. In his article "Jubilee in Leviticus 17-26" Jerome C. Ross examines the concept of Jubilee and concludes that "the Jubilee regulations are the developments of the principle of Sabbath, which is designed for control and management of the economics of the community."[5] He further states that one of the implications of the practice of Jubilee in modern life is that "people should not profit at the expense of others' integrity. Economic exploitation is tabooed!"[6]

Now it is quite clear why this Jubilee emphasis is ignored. The political-economic system of capitalism that the developed world practices and that we Black Christians have uncritically accepted is rooted in the exploitation of others. Our history as slaves ought to be our example. However, we remain woefully ignorant of the true nature of chattel slavery as practiced in America.

Slavery was not a mere inconvenience as some would have us think. It was a brutal form of exploitation that used the labor of Blacks to enrich Whites. It was not a random system, but an incremental, planned, public policy that began as early as 1638 when the Maryland Colonist Assembly passed the first public edict stating that the original 20 free Blacks "nor their offspring shall be permitted to enjoy the fruits of white society."[7] By 1665 this edict had been adopted throughout the colonies as part of slave codes to ensure that Blacks would be an "available, uncompensated, noncompetitive, well-disciplined, permanently subordinated work force, [to] be separated from the white society."[8] This public policy was supported by government laws, social institutions (including the church), and general practices of Whites. Exploited labor is the engine of capitalism and the underpinning of the American stock market and its prosperity. Furthermore, it is anathema to the Gospel Jesus proclaimed and the Jubilee text He read.

In the latter part of Isaiah 61, God promises that ruined cities would be repaired, devastations would be cleared and rebuilt, and that Israelites would enjoy the wealth of the nations and receive a double portion for the shame they endured. It is no stretch of the imagination to assume that this was in the minds of the people and a focus of the Good News Jesus addressed. When He finished reading, He proclaimed that the scripture was fulfilled in their hearing. In other words, Jesus proclaimed that Jubilee had begun. The people understood and "spoke well of him" because the new age and a new economic order were at hand. However, when He told them it would not be limited to their societal circle, they tried to throw Him off a cliff.

Each phrase of that initial sermon has been over-spiritualized and needs to be reexamined. Jesus emphasizes the release of the captives. The captives are those whose lives are completely controlled and constrained by others. The captives are the prisoners of war who are locked in slavery because their side lost. That was the custom of that day. They could be freed, but only if some one paid for them or they were rescued in another war.

Also, the captives are those who have been sold to pay off family debts. Sometimes theses unfortunate persons would be thrown into the debtors' prison. These are the trapped whom later we are commissioned to visit (Matthew 25: 31-46).

Other captives are the demon possessed. We know from biblical descriptions that this group is plagued by a variety of ailments, including mental illness, epilepsy, and addiction.

The captive is illustrated in the Gospels by the man named legion, Mary Magdalene who was possessed by seven demons, and the boy who foamed at the mouth. They are trapped by behavior over which they have little or no control. These examples of captives directly relate to our own era and afflictions as a people.

Prisons exist in America, and the majority of prisoners are Black. What war did they lose that caused them to be prisoners? Certainly it was not one of the wars in which America was involved. We have been the most loyal of groups, having fought on behalf of this country in every war, including the Revolution. We did not lose the Civil War even though most of us lived in the South. Besides, we do not take prisoners as prizes of war anymore, or do we?

Perhaps these prisoners are a result of the economic wars we have lost. The fact that the majority of Black Americans live in impoverished neighborhoods is an indicator that we have lost some kind of war. The lack of political clout and ownership (property, business, etc.) in our communities (or anywhere else for that matter) are indicators that we are controlled by others, so we must have lost some war. Losers become economic prisoners and simple fuel for someone else's system. "I have come to set the captive free" very much applies to us in the 21st century.

There are no debtors' prisons anymore; however, there is a captive class. Debt and the constraints it puts on our behavior is very much present. We constantly fight the battle of good sense vs. consumerism. We are assaulted everyday to buy the latest, the sexiest, the coolest, the newest "flava" of the month. Whether a gadget or clothing, many of us have succumbed and are captive to the endless

An Awesome Declaration

cycle of material chains. Even those who have jumped off the cycle of credit card debt find a very real bill still facing us every month. It alters our lifestyle and affects our ability to be effective in our work for the Kingdom.

Because we are no longer slaves, segregation is no longer legal, and we are continually told how much the Black middleclass has grown, it is hard to see the existence of a captive class. Looming on the horizon, though, is a large group of young adults with student loans coming due. Already the number of medical practitioners has dropped significantly as fewer students can afford the cost of medical school.

Addictive behavior is at an all–time high in our society despite or perhaps because of the relative wealth we have in this country. However, the cause is the same that precipitated the ancient captive: We have no purpose or mission that drives us, inspires us, or governs our waking moments. Therefore, we are simply tossed about whimsically and at will. We are caught in a web, serving someone else's ignoble purpose and living so much beneath the purpose for which we were created.

There is a third group, the blind. This term, "the blind," is often used both literally and figuratively throughout the Gospels. There is only one case where Jesus heals a blind man directly and that is in Mark 10: 46-52 and Luke 18: 35-42. (Most scholars think that Matthew 20: 29-34 refers to the same incident although it refers to two men.) In the Gospel of Mark he is named Bartimaeus. His healing comes about through his persistence and at the word of Jesus. Once healed, the beggar praises God and the crowd responds likewise.

As R. Alan Culpepper states in his commentary on Luke in *The New Interpreter's Bible*, "The healing of the blind man carries important theological freight here."[9] Clearly this miracle is a fulfillment of Jesus' sermon at Nazareth and is meant for interpretation broader than the limits of physical healing. There is a legitimate spiritual and figurative sight that God desires for His people. To put it another way, Bartimaeus once healed is no longer as dependent an individual as he was before. He is no longer as vulnerable to the abuses of others. He is made whole and can function as a human being with new vitality. He praises God. The crowd praises God.

The poignant question for us is, How many persons would praise God if we as a people received our sight with a new sense of mission and purpose so that we were no longer led by those who do not have our best interest at heart? Would there be rejoicing and praising God if we were able to function much more independently as consumers, voters, parents, and as a people? There are many who have a vested interest in keeping us without a clear sense of purpose and mission and therefore blind and dependent.

Although I have presented a figurative interpretation, we cannot ignore the physical Jesus' healing and its implied message that God is concerned about our physical ailments. This is good news. We as a people lead the nation in heart disease, diabetes, stroke, high blood pressure, AIDS/HIV, and other sexually transmitted diseases (STDs). Sickle cell, asthma, cancer, and the like result in life expectancy rates that are significantly shorter than other groups of Americans.

These basic facts are fairly well publicized. Much less publicized is the low number of doctors who practice in the Black community, the unavailability of quality health insurance, and the racism that exists in the practice and administration of medicine, resulting in substandard treatment. A God that is concerned about our physical ailments and conditions is indeed good news.

The final group addressed by Jesus is the oppressed. Most commentators link this group to the first, the poor, and rightly so. Today, we would call them the working poor, the low–wage worker who holds two and three jobs and works six, sometimes seven, days a week. The oppressed are also the harried and the anxious who see little point in living beyond the daily grind. The good news is that there is relief not only at the spiritual and emotional levels but there is also relief from dire economic situations.

It is clear from this quick review of Jesus' initial sermon in Nazareth that important parts of the Gospel have been underemphasized. There is no emphasis on the "saving of souls" as we generally mean it. In Luke 12: 15-20 Jesus challenges a young man about greed and reminds him that there are greater things to focus on, e.g., the state of one's soul vs. the state of one's possessions. However, neither Jesus nor His disciples move about asking people if they are "saved." In fact, the term "saved" is seldom mentioned in the four Gospels.

What is repeated over and over is the link between meeting concrete needs and true spirituality. Jesus says it best when He describes the final judgment scene in Matthew 25: 31-46: *When did we see you hungry or thirsty or a stranger or naked or sick or in prison and did not minister to you? Truly, I tell you, just as you did not do it to one of the least of these you did not do it to me.* There is a scathing indictment of our "saved theology" in these words.

On the other hand, the concreteness of Jesus' Good News message is an awesome declaration. It challenges the lip service of our churches, and its relevance to our contemporary times is both liberating and disconcerting. How we go about working for the fulfillment of this Jubilee decree determines whether our people will see a more equitable reality and even determines the well–being of our souls.

THE STRANGE AND UNUSUAL GOOD NEWS

One day, while he was teaching, Phari-sees and teachers of the Law were sitting near-by (they had come from every village of Galilee and Judea and from Jerusalem); and the power of the Lord was with him to heal. Just then some men came, carrying a paralyzed man on a bed. They were trying to bring him in and lay him before Jesus; but finding no way to bring him in because of the crowd, they went up on the roof and let him down with his bed through the tiles into the middle of the crowd in front of Jesus. When He saw their faith, He said, "Friend, your sins are forgiven you." Then the scribes and the Pharisees began to question, "Who is this who is speaking blasphemies? Who can forgive sins but God alone?" When Jesus perceived their questionings, He answered them, "Why do you raise such questions in your hearts? Which is easier, to say, 'Your sins are forgiven you,' or to say, 'Stand up and walk'? But so that you may know that the Son of Man has authority on earth to forgive sins"—he said to the one who was paralyzed—"I say to you, stand up and take your bed and go to your home." Immediately

he stood up before them, took what he had been lying on, and went to his home, glorifying God. Amazement seized all of them, and they glorified God and were filled with awe, saying, "We have seen strange things today."

Luke 5: 17-26

Before we rush on, there is another facet of the Good News message that must be discussed: concern for the soul and the problem of sin. We normally understand sin as a highly personalized fault or weakness. It is also benignly called "a missing of the mark." Sin is thought of as a violation of the easy "thou shalt nots"—murder, steal, have illicit sex, drink, forget the Sabbath.

Our concept of sin is damaging but not devastating. It is the object of our temptation or, at best, a thorn in the flesh. Sometimes sin expands to a greater context, but only in the most horrendous cases. We have been taught that sin stains our soul and jeopardizes our place in heaven. Beyond that, in the postmodern world we live in, there is little consequence to sin in our minds.

The healing event recorded in Luke 5: 17-26 is generally interpreted as a miracle story. However, the healing event is better seen as an example story, a teaching tool for the church. Though I use the Luke version, this story was originally recorded in the Gospel of Mark. Both versions along with Matthew's parallel text are substantially the

The Strange and Unusual Good News

same. Luke and Mark report that a crowd had gathered in the house where Jesus was teaching. However, Luke emphasizes that this crowd consists mainly of Pharisees and teachers of the Law. They come from every village of Galilee and Judea and even from Jerusalem. They are not there for miracles or healing. They are there for debate and discussion.

The Pharisees and scribes have gathered from all the towns to hear Jesus teach and discuss among themselves. It sounds like a conference, seminar, or church convention, where there is little expectation beyond discussion and fellowship. Two things stand out in this example story.

First, although Jesus is there to teach, He also has the power to heal. This is not revealed to the crowd until a man shows up in great need. There is a man in need, gross need. He is paralyzed and unable to help himself without great assistance. His condition makes it very difficult for him to work harder or pull himself up by his own bootstraps. His condition is such that the easy answers will not do. The party line or the cultural mythology will not solve his problem. He is paralyzed, locked in what is a seemingly irreversible condition.

The Pharisees and teachers of the Law have gathered to debate and discuss. Since they are religious leaders, one would assume that they would discuss this man's condition, but that is not the case. This confab of religious leaders left on their own will accomplish little. This is no different from many of our conferences about Black America. Whether it is a secular or a religious gathering, however well intentioned, action is seldom taken. Meanwhile, Black people lie in a paralyzed state of poverty, economic deprivation, poor health care, and disease.

This is not so much an indictment as a description of the normal state of our churches and other institutions. Those not afflicted have a lot to say about those who are, but little action follows. This perpetual state of inertia has a long history. It is not just the malady of a postmodern age. Those who were the original readers probably had no trouble relating to this Bible story of potentially insignificant outcome, and neither should we.

But then the story takes an unexpected turn. Something strange and unusual happens. Friends work together to bring their paralyzed companion to where he might receive aid. Finding the way blocked, they regroup and come up with an out- of- the- box strategy. Go through the roof. Once there, they proceed to remove the tiles. Mark's description is more dramatic, for he says they dig their way through the roof and lower the man to the feet of Jesus.

Make no mistake, organized effort on behalf of one who is helpless and written off as hopeless is strange and highly unusual. The kind of perseverance demonstrated by these anonymous men is nothing short of miraculous and noteworthy even to God. Luke puts it this way: "When He saw their faith, Jesus said, 'Friend, your sins are forgiven.'" At this point, the religious leaders spring into action with

loud objections. Jesus' pronouncement about the forgiveness of sin is not in line with their thinking or their doctrine. They are not just a little disturbed, they are furious.

Then a challenge is issued: "Which is easier, to say,
'Your sins are forgiven you' or 'Stand up and walk'"? The
religious leaders respond with silence. Jesus was asking
them a "put up or shut up" question. He was asking them
to go beyond the debate to a substantial act.

There are a host of questions that consume us as religious leaders and laity. Who has or does not have the Holy
Spirit? What is the authentic religion of the Black man?
Who has a full gospel or half gospel? Are we praying and
praising properly? There is no end to the self-help books,
spiritual growth manuals, and the like, but cut to the chase.

The real issue, the most pressing question is, Does our
belief have any teeth to it? Can our faith actually make a
difference in this real world? Not a psychological or symbolic difference, but a dramatic difference? The question
Jesus posed to the Pharisees and scribes is still relevant to
the Black Church: Is it more important to get the doctrine
correct or to meet the needs that challenge our people? The
silence is deafening.

In response to the silence of the Pharisees and scribes,
Jesus speaks and acts. *So that you may know that the Son
of Man has authority on earth to forgive sins,* He says, and
then turns to the paralyzed man and commands him to stand
up, take up his bed, and go home, which the man promptly
does. Let's rephrase what Jesus says. "So that you might

understand the true nature of God, His concern and power to hit the mark, rise up and take up your bed and go home."

The religious leaders had missed the mark. They had "sinned." They came with no expectation other than to debate and discuss; there was absolutely no expectation of radical change or healing. They did not really believe in God's power or His concern about human suffering. The man and his friends came with that expectation. For some reason they believed that if they could get their friend in the house, Jesus could make a difference. They believed that Jesus indeed had the power to affect their friend's condition. It was this faith that caused the group to focus on getting the job done. Get to Jesus. As I stated at the outset, this is more than an amazing miracle story. The cry of the crowd was "We have seen strange things." What they saw was something out of the ordinary.

It is indeed strange and unusual when anything really is accomplished or changed by our doctrinal discussions. While our discussions, Bible studies, revivals, conferences, conventions, and seminars do make a distinct difference in the values we hold and lives we live and affect, the healing of the paralyzed man begs the question, What more can *we* do? Do we really expect that the Gospel will make a difference in our condition right here, right now, or are our voices individually and collectively bantering in the wind? Are we missing the mark? When people leave our gatherings, will they be filled with awe saying, "We have seen strange things," or will they say, "We saw the same old thing. We had church."

The Gospel message is not simply about an abstract, individualistic faith. Faith is a collective power. Luke and Mark comment that what moved Jesus was the faith of these friends. This faith was exhibited in their collective action. From the original idea, to organizing, through perseverance and final innovation, these friends united around one goal: get their friend to Jesus. That is faith that can be seen.

You cannot separate faith from action. *Faith without works is dead* (James 2: 26b). Action or "works," involves planning, thought, improvisation, and perseverance. This may be an unsettling thought, but perhaps that is precisely why more is not accomplished and we miss the mark. We sin when we become complacent in our expectations and therefore cannot help but do less than what is needed for new miracles to occur.

To serve the present age,

My calling to fulfill,

O may it all my powers engage

To do my Master's will.

FROM DELUSION TO SANITY

They came to the other side of the sea, to the country of the Gerasenes. And when He had stepped out of the boat, immediately a man out of the tombs with an unclean spirit met Him. He lived among the tombs; and no one could restrain him any more, even with a chain; for he had often been restrained with shackles and chains, but the chains he wrenched apart, and the shackles he broke in pieces; and no one had the strength to subdue him. Night and day among the tombs and on the mountains he was always howling and bruising himself with stones. When he saw Jesus from a distance, he ran and bowed down before Him; and he shouted at the top of his voice, "What have you to do with me, Jesus, Son of the Most High God? I adjure you by God, do not torment me." For He had said to him, "Come out of the man, you unclean spirit!" Then Jesus asked him, "What is your name?" He replied, "My name is Legion; for we are many." He begged Him earnestly not to send them out of the country. Now there on the hillside a great herd of swine was feeding; and the unclean spirits begged Him, "Send us into

the swine; let us enter them." So He gave them permission. And the unclean spirits came out and entered the swine; and the herd, numbering about two thousand, rushed down the steep bank into the sea, and were drowned in the sea.

The swineherds ran off and told it in the city and in the country. Then people came to see what it was that had happened. They came to Jesus and saw the demoniac sitting there, clothed and in his right mind, the very man who had had the legion; and they were afraid. Those who had seen what had happened to the demoniac and to the swine reported it. Then they began to beg Jesus to leave their neighborhood. As he was getting into the boat, the man who had been possessed by demons begged him that he might be with him. But Jesus refused, and said to him, "Go home to your friends, and tell them how much the Lord has done for you, and what mercy he has shown you." And he went away and began to proclaim in the Decapolis how much Jesus had done for him; and everyone was amazed.

Mark 5: 1-15

Early biblical scholars regarded the Gospel of Mark as the least theological of the four Gospels and more of a simple recounting of the deeds of Jesus. Modern scholars now realize that in its simplicity, Mark is also a highly theological document. Mark is the first of the Gospel writers to explain the universal significance of the life, death, and resurrection of Jesus of Nazareth, the unique Son of God. The shortest of the four Gospels, Mark provides the most detailed account of Jesus' encounter with this madman of the tombs. Almost mythic in style, this narrative is hauntingly surreal in its contemporary interpretation.

We know this man of Gerasene. He is the big kid who hung on the corner and took your lunch money before graduating to larger crime. He smoked cigarettes before anyone else. He was first to drink and do drugs. As kids we laughed when we heard him scream from being beaten with an ironing cord (the old kind, thick with crude insulation). We ran when we came outside, knowing he would "kick our butts" if he caught us. Before mainstreaming became the norm, he was in the "special" class. We did not regard him as retarded. This was crazy Leon. We know this man of Gerasene. He is called hardcore in the rap world now, and before that he was a thug, a gangbanger, a bad boy. He was Richard Wright's Bigger Thomas. During slavery, the master made an example of this "bad nigger" to keep the slaves in check.

We know him because he is thoroughly part of American mythology. He is the substance of White men's nightmares, White women's fantasies, and the lost branch of the upwardly mobile Black family. We know this man of

Gerasene. Black as midnight, this illusion of a man lives in a deluded state.

Since we know this man of Gerasene, let us not fail to look beyond the surface of the story for he serves a useful function. He is the town bogeyman. One can almost hear the townspeople of Mark's day telling their children, "Stay out of that cemetery, and don't go in those mountains. The madman will get you!" "Eat all your food so you can be strong enough to run from him." "Obey your parents and get home before dark because he is out there." Frightened and curious, like all children, they questioned their parents. "What's he like, mama?" "Oh no man can hold him. He has broken shackles and chains. Why even our strongest men cannot subdue him."

In 1992, five Los Angeles policemen stopped a Black man who they alleged ran a stoplight and was high on drugs. The officers beat him 75 times. He was maced, stungunned, and handcuffed, but the police still claimed he was guilty of resisting arrest. The entire incident was caught on videotape, and Rodney King became the center of a news spectacle.

At his trial the officers were acquitted by an all White jury, and many throughout the nation were outraged, particularly in Black America. But do we really understand what took place? The jury did not see Rodney King, the man. Their decision was based on an illusion: Rodney King, the super–predator, the drugged big Black man, the childhood bogeyman of White America, the madman of

From Delusion to Sanity

Gerasene. The White jury saw a Black man who not only, supposedly, challenged the authority of police, but they also saw in Rodney King the embodiment of their childhood fears.

Since the Rodney King acquittal, other incidents have occurred. Little has changed. White America still fears the madman of Gerasene.

Fear of the Black bogeyman serves a useful function in our society. Little White boys and girls can imitate him and make their rebellion statement. Sixty–six percent of the rap records sold are bought by a young White audience.[10] Eminem, the White rapper, talks and acts like a Black man.

Money flows into the coffers of security firms because of the Black bogeyman. Politicians locally and nationally get elected because of him. The black bogeyman is behind those pledges to get tough on crime. Willie Horton was instrumental in George Herbert Walker Bush being elected president.

We as Black Christians cannot be naive and ignore the fact that this fear operates in our society. We also must confess that we know it and have used that childhood fear to our advantage, personally and collectively. Intimidation and intimation go a long way. I have watched Black kids in prep schools intimidate White kids by imitating the language of the streets, complete with requisite body language. Intimated beneath the upper–middleclass buppie exterior is that dangerous Black person, waiting to jump out if you are not careful.

Yet we delude ourselves if we think there is real power in this image. In Mark the narrator notes that the man of Gerasene spent all night and day wandering and howling among the tombs. While the noise scared the children and townspeople, he never harmed anyone other than himself. He cuts and bruises his own body. There is no real fear of the madman. Childhood fear is one thing; adult fear is something else altogether. There is no adult fear of the madman of Gerasene. He just makes noise.

There is no real adult fear of the Willie Hortons, Rodney Kings, or gangsta rapper mugging on the video. Three–strike laws were passed without a veto by then president Bill Clinton. Mr. Clinton also failed to rectify sentencing disparities for crack possession vs. cocaine possession, and still some Black leaders call him the first Black president. "Bad boys," some 1.3 million, have turned a good profit for others serving as the economic engines and political leverage for depressed White communities where public and private prisons are built. Felony convictions cause Black men to lose their right to vote, and yet their numbers can be used in the census for congressional redistricting, even while incarcerated.

Sadly, we have been remiss in recognizing that there is no power in thugism. It serves only to cut and bruise our own Black society. Crime statistics consistently reveal that most of the crimes committed by Black people are against other Black people. This is not new news. Staying safe in our own neighborhoods from our own people remains a disturbing challenge. But there is a greater challenge for Black Christians to consider.

As self-destructive and deluded as this man of Gerasene is, when he encounters Jesus, he quickly makes his way along the road from delusion to sanity. The challenge is to travel that same road. What do I mean? Look closer.

When this man of Gerasene encounters Jesus he cries out, "Do not torment me," for he sees Jesus as one who has come to confront his deluded state. Do we see an encounter with Jesus as a confrontation with our delusional state? Popular religious doctrine does not recognize this reality. We say Jesus will "save your soul." What we mean by that I am never really sure, but it usually has little to do with here and now and much to do with our place in heaven hereafter.

We do say Jesus will redeem you from sin, which is confrontation, but that sin is relegated to a few choice behaviors: alcoholism, drug use, illicit sex (the definition of this has become fuzzy, so there is less emphasis on that particular sin), theft, assault, murder, and hating White people—a great sin. Hating White people is one sin we will not tolerate in the Black Christian community. We are constantly reminded that we are to love everybody, especially White people and others that do not look like us. Meanwhile, self-hatred or hating Black people barely cause a ripple in the bond of our psyche. We repeat the admonition to love everybody like a mantra, but we ignore

Jesus' admonition to love one another. To paraphrase I John 4: 20, How can we love everybody we cannot see and not love our Black brothers and sisters whom we do see every day?

Does an encounter with Jesus force a confrontation? In our society tolerance has become the watchword and one of the highest values of a "spiritual" person. Shame and guilt have become great evils to be avoided. Black Christians are not immune to this influence and have adopted the same value system.

Confrontation in any substantial way has passed from our religious demeanor. We think Jesus wants to be our buddy, not our exorcist. Never mind that to be our friend He might have to appear as tormentor, especially when we have sunk to a deluded and dysfunctional state. We are more like the man of Gerasene than we wish to admit, for he had adapted completely to living the life of a bogeyman. Conversely, we have adapted to being non-troublemakers, minstrels, and non-Black leaders in our quest to be "successful" Christians.

Yet, unlike the man of Gerasene, our delusions remain hidden to us even when we encounter Jesus. The madman knew he was in a sad, complex, delusional state. When asked his name or to describe himself, he replied, "My name is Legion, for we are many."

Perhaps the greatest challenge for us is to recognize the complexity of the illusions we have come to accept.

From Delusion to Sanity

For example, since 1994 almost 70 percent of Black children have been born to single–parent households. This has become our norm. Baby dedications are now attended by one parent or grandparent with no father present. In a gathering of 30 Black Christian women (there was a cross–section of ages), it was discovered after some discussion about relationships, that only two were married.

In weddings the norm is for the children of the couple to serve as flower girls and ring bearers. We seldom mention the abnormality of this and pretend it's OK. A community cannot exist when 70 percent of its children are born into families that have no male role models in the household and no sharing of child–rearing responsibilities.

Economically, single parenting is a formula for poverty and heartache. Not that there are no exceptions. Some persons have done it and done it well. But most flounder in their struggle to raise their children. Our statistics for lack of child support are appalling. What will this mean for succeeding generations? Black Christians seldom address this question. We do not want to make anyone feel guilty or ashamed, but in our efforts to be tolerant, we are hurting our community today, and we are creating a legion of problems for future generations, our children.

The recent uproar about the Catholic Church turning a blind eye to priests who sexually molested children will pale in comparison to revelations of Black churches complicity. We have failed to confront the irresponsible behaviors (lack of child support, alcoholism, drug use, illicit sex, etc.) that exist in our churches and neighborhoods and that have caused widespread socioeconomic trauma in the Black community.

There are many other complex delusions that have robbed us of our sanity. We must begin to move from delusion to sanity if we are to heal the chronic ills in our community.

The last verses of Mark's text raise more interesting issues about sanity. I stated earlier that childhood fear and adult fear are two different phenomena. In the text the children's fear is assumed, but the adult fear is clearly stated. The people express their fear and beg Jesus to leave them after the madman of Gerasene is healed, clothed, and in his right mind—and two thousand pigs have been destroyed.

It is interesting to note that the writer is very detailed in his description of the madman and the context, but there is no mention of fear until the economic disaster is experienced by the townspeople and they see the man clothed and in his right mind. Then fear takes hold. At least two comments are appropriate here. Economic rearrangements always garner attention and what is it about being in one's right mind that provokes such fear?

The economic rearrangement, or disaster, is told in detail. It is caused by the evil spirits entering the herd of swine, unclean animals to Jews, and their subsequent plunge off a cliff into the sea. This might have been humorous to the original Jewish readers since they viewed pigs as unclean animals. They probably felt that the Gentile owners deserved the large economic loss that came from a herd of two thousand perishing.

This detail suggests that the healing took place in Gentile territory. Perhaps though, something else was being alluded to. This region, according to Luke and confirmed by Josephus, was ruled by Phillip, the brother of Herod Antipas and the son of Herod the Great, who began the rebuilding of the temple in Jerusalem. Phillip was at least a nominal Jew with Idumean roots. Like his father, Phillip was appointed by Rome to rule this largely Gentile territory. He built the cities of Caesarea Philippi and Bethesda that figured prominently in the ministry of Jesus. Most of the persons in this territory were Gentile, but not all. Some were Jews and Samaritans who also practiced the Law. Phillip was in good graces with Rome and would later be highly regarded by his subjects. Because of this curious relationship of Jewish king over Gentile and Jewish subjects, I will share the following experience.

While touring Israel a few years ago, our tour bus stopped at the market store of a Kibbutz. It was well stocked with European and American foods and had a fresh deli counter. The tour guide remarked that all of the deli meats were fresh from the Kibbutz. We were surprised because the selection included a variety of hams. When we remarked about it, he was quite candid. Pigs were raised on the Kibbutz to ship mainly to Italy, where the market was very lucrative. The Jewish farmers had come to disregard that aspect of kosher law and had themselves acquired a taste for ham on the Kibbutz.

Human nature being what it is, I am sure this was not the first time that dietary laws were compromised because of the marketplace. Perhaps in this case Mark was alluding to a practice in this territory of Jews or Samaritans raising the "unclean" animals for sale to this largely Gentile population, or perhaps he was making a more political statement against the syncretism of Phillip that inevitably had to take place. Certainly there was the precedent of John the Baptist, commenting fervently against the practice of Phillip's brother, Herod Antipas. This of course is speculation, but what is to be noted is the relationship between the economic rearrangement and the salvation of this madman. We like to ignore such connections, but they cannot be ignored.

Fear comes over the people as this man now sits clothed and in his right mind. Clothed means his appearance has been transformed. He is no longer readily identifiable as an outsider or a madman. Even his scars of self-mutilation are covered. He can no longer be distinguished from the "civilized" people. He can now be one of them.

This causes us to reflect on two levels. When their appearance changes, the madmen cannot be distinguished from the norm. Appearances are a basis for judgment and afford us some opportunities that would not come our way in the general society. In our Black social hierarchy, and there is still very much one, the thug can be hidden by appearance. Better yet, what distinguishes us from each other is only appearance, unless there is some mark such as a tattoo that is uncoverable. Our young naively think that those body piercings do not matter. They do matter, they really do.

The second level is much more disconcerting. We Black folk can change our apparel, but the blessing of our melanin still makes us distinguishable. This is disconcerting for those who want to blend in. For them it is a reality that can be laborious to live with. Ellis Cose's book *Rage of the Privileged Class* is a documentary on this reality. In it a successful businessman says that despite having done everything right, he is still regarded as an interloper having to prove himself.[11]

What does it mean to be in one's right mind? Why does this evoke so much fear? To say it another way, the townspeople feared sanity more than insanity. It is astonishing. They were not afraid of the man living in a delusional state, yet when they find him acting in a reasoned and rational manner they are fearful.

Some rather unsettling implications surface. To be in one's right mind can simply mean to be rational and reasonable. A rational and reasonable mind asks questions and demands answers. A rational and reasonable mind will not be swayed by emotional appeal only. A sane mind will upset the proverbial applecart because much of our societal behavior is predicated on accepting a certain amount of unsubstantiated half–truths, inadequate information, unreasoned prejudice, self–serving assumptions, and decision making based on pure emotional appeal. Emotional appeals coupled with a certain human resistance to behavioral change ensure that the paradigms of our civil society rarely undergo radical shifts in perception.

In interpreting the Mark 5 story in light of our situation as Black people, it would be easy to focus on White America's childlike fears of Blacks, but let us not begin there. Let us start with the adult fear of a sane and reasonable mind that does not respond to simple emotional appeal or societal mythology. In other words, what does it mean for us to be clothed in our right mind? If this is the measuring rod, are we up to the challenge or are we fearful? And why?

To be clothed in one's right mind is to demand accountability from our leadership. By and large, we as Blacks have not demanded accountability on any consistent basis. It has not happened in our church conventions, not from our so-called spokespersons, nor from our elected officials. We settle too easily for melodramatic emotionalism or cerebral fluff. Every September the Congressional Black Caucus holds it brain trust, seminars, and meetings, but little follow–up is ever demonstrated or demanded. The year-to-year follow up in our church conventions, fraternal organizations, and civil rights groups is no better. The indictment that the Mark text levels is not just against White society; uncomfortably, it begins with us.

We must confront the delusions that we Black folk have accepted. Selling bean pies, incense, and newspapers in the middle of traffic on a hot July day while dressed in suit and bow tie is neither a definition of meaningful work nor the product of a reasonable mind. Neither is the passive acceptance of every Black figure that parades in front of us as a spokesperson or leader. Most of all, if the Gospel we preach and respond to as a people only demands accountability for worship attendance and the volume and fervor of our praise, then we have deluded ourselves and missed the high calling of Jesus Christ.

White America has an irrational fear of Black people. I write this not out of rage or anger but as a simple statement of fact. Not all White people are afraid of us, but most are.

Some years ago, a White colleague related an incident from when he traveled on the Boston subway (the T). He got off at the wrong stop and ended up in Jamaica Plain. As he stepped off the train and started down the steps, he said he froze, for as far as he could see there were Black people. He said he was uncomfortable.

The truth was he was scared. No one had bothered him, spoken to him, or threatened him. He simply saw a sea of Black people and realized that he was alone, and the childlike fear kicked in. He said, "I guess this is how Black people feel when they walk about in our society." I informed him no, only those who have not spent any time around White people. Many Blacks have perfected the nondescript smile and movements that placate Whites and their fears of behavior that might be misinterpreted as aggressive. The "we are just like you" handbook has been studied so that in all our interaction we can allay latent childlike fears. At most, we feel annoyed to participate in the ritual as a lone Black in a White crowd.

But there is more to it than that. One of the irrational assumptions is that to be pro-Black is to be anti-White. To have an appreciation of what God has done through and with us as a Black people is anathema to many of us. We keep trying to serve everyone. It is telling that in scripture when the reclaimed madman wants to leave the fearful, civilized folk and follow Jesus, he is told to stay and go into that environment and tell his friends what the Lord did for him. In other words, now that you have been awakened and are in your right mind, go and wake up your friends also.

We have a legitimate message for our own community that no one else can tell. There are some delusions and inappropriate behaviors among us that can only be changed if we confront and hold each other accountable and share our own testimony of deliverance from delusion to sanity.

Those that have ears, let them hear.

WHERE IS THE FIRE?

O Lord, you have enticed me, and I was enticed;
You have overpowered me, and you have prevailed.
I have become a laughingstock all day long;
Everyone mocks me.
For whenever I speak, I must cry out,
I must shout, "Violence and destruction!"
For the word of the Lord has become for me
A reproach and derision all day long.
If I say, "I will not mention him, or speak any more in his name,"
Then within me there is something like a burning fire
Shut up in my bones;
I am weary with holding it in, and I cannot.

                              Jeremiah 20: 7-9 NRSV

Like a burning fire shut up in my bones is one of the better-known phrases in the writings of Jeremiah. Unfortunately, it has become one of the most trivialized texts of the modern Black Church. Though quoted often in sermons and in many gospel songs, the power of this text lies largely dormant. If one should desire to get a few amens, read this text when called upon to choose a scripture. Such is the power of its imagery. If one desires more than a few amen's read this text with a hint of the singsong rhythm of an old country preacher, and the congregational response is even more vocal in affirmation. However, that by and large is where it ends.

Is this simply another text suffering from lack of relevant interpretation, or is there something more at stake? Why should we be concerned? As we examine the causes of the trivialization of this text and the loss of meaning and its consequences, we will indeed discover that the rescue of the Black Church and our people from the malaise that infects us is at stake.

Let us look first at the imagery itself, *like a burning fire shut up in my bones*. Jeremiah uses an extremely powerful image that has lost a great deal of potency because of a cultural shift. Few of us regularly encounter fire. Cooking, once done on a wood–burning stove, is now done on electric or gas ranges. The charcoal grill for the weekend cookout still exists, but it is quickly losing ground to outdoor propane grills. The fireplace exists for some but not for the majority of us. We are no longer an agricultural community, so we do not see fire used to clear fields of last year's crops or bonfires of stumps and old trees.

The visual image of a fire with its various hues of yellow, red, orange, and even blue is lost to us because it is not part of our modern world. Not so in Jeremiah's day. Fire was part of their daily lives, and its inherent dangers

Where Is the Fire?

and power were well known. The pungent smell of a fire was routine, while for us it is rarely experienced. We are more familiar with the sound of a fire engine than the amazing pop and crackle of a roaring fire, to say nothing of the mini-explosions that take place in an inferno.

The heat from a fire is lost to us. A hot fire can literally peal the skin back before the flames actually make contact. I learned this working one summer in an alloy mill. Long underwear and long–sleeve shirts were worn to keep the heat away from your body, for the heat itself was damaging.

Unless one is a fireman, we seldom experience the ravaging power and uncontrollable nature of a fire. Because of TV, we are able to see a fire in progress, but video is a cool medium that does little to convey the chaotic and frenzied nature of a fire. We hear news reports of multi-alarm blazes that take five, six, or nine hours to bring under control and think nothing of it. What is really being reported is that for four, five, or eight hours the fire was in charge, going where it wanted to go with a degree of unpredictability that put the firefighters in mortal danger and relegated surrounding buildings to the role of fuel.

In Jeremiah's day fire was a weapon of war. To lay siege to a city and then set it on fire was an act of immense cruelty. To unleash fire on a surrounded people was a cruel and cursed act. It was also a volatile act, for a shift of wind could turn the weapon meant for the enemy into an ally of the enemy, as the fire turned upon those who set it.

We have none of these raw, powerful images to draw on in our modern database of similies. In one sense we cannot help but be detached and unmoved when the term "fire" is used as a symbol. The one area that has some feel to it is when we refer to sexual desires as fire, such as the fire of passion. We have some reference for metaphors such as "my burning heart," etc.

Consequently, with this sole frame of reference, we interpret the imagery of Jeremiah's phrase "like a burning fire shut up in my bones" as little more than the flush of so much testosterone or estrogen, which rapidly increases the blood flow in certain organs. While not discounting the power of sexual desire, it is tame in comparison to the powerful imagery Jeremiah had in mind, and trivial when we recontextualize this image into our faith walk.

A once popular gospel song serves as a good example.

It's like fire shut up in my bones
Like Jeremiah won't leave me alone
I'm going to sing to the power of the Lord comes down.
Won't let Satan turn me around

The imagery has little power or potency to it. It may make us want to sing. Songs can be a mild form of protest, though lacking the power of Jeremiah's utterance. Devoid of a contextual reference, our subsequent interpretation and application is devoid of relevance and trivial in scope.

Where Is the Fire?

Let's look at the context of these verses. They are taken from the last personal laments that Jeremiah makes to God. His contention is that God has suckered him by calling him to a prophetic task. The result of his obedience is that he is beaten, whipped, and put on public display in a high–traffic area. Jeremiah is tortured and publicly humiliated by his enemies, and he indicts God as a co-conspirator. After all, it is God who has called him to this prophetic task and God who urged Jeremiah to proclaim the Lord's message on the temple steps. Furthermore, when Jeremiah tries to resign from his post as prophet, he finds that he cannot. He has been commissioned by God to proclaim "the Word." The way to resign is to keep silent, and therefore not carry out his assignment. But he finds he cannot. Despite the pain of his physical and psychic scars, Jeremiah cannot keep silent.

The "fire shut up in my bones" impedes him from carrying out his logical and sensible resolve to keep silent. Certainly, this is more than a resolve to whistle a happy tune in the midst of a storm or sing a song of protest in an oppressive situation. There is a violent, raging inferno residing deep inside Jeremiah. It is deeper than flesh; it is in the marrow of his bones. What Jeremiah poetically describes is a phenomenon that has disappeared from the context of our modern life. More disturbing, it has disappeared from our concept of religion and what it means to walk with God.

A CHALLENGE TO THE BLACK CHURCH

What has disappeared is the prophetic rage that could not be separated from Jeremiah and who he was. This is what Jeremiah poetically describes as a fire deep within. Jeremiah had this inner outrage and a passionate concern about righteousness, but not in the abstract. He could not keep his vow of silence, for this inner turmoil, this prophetic rage would not let him turn his eyes away from the corrupt behaviors of his people. He could not turn away from the horrifying practice of parents sacrificing their children for the sake of their own comfort, all under the guise of religion. Nor could he ignore the ruthless business practices and unjust legal practices nor the distrust and cynicism that were part of the everyday life situations of his people (9:4).

These things do not just simply bother Jeremiah. They cause rage inside of him. This is not an ordinary rage but a heated skin–peeling, pungent–smelling, roaring, consuming, explosive reaction that forces him to override the primal instinct of self–preservation and the human ego's need to save face. His poetic confession reveals that he is the loser in a battle of wills, and he is ultimately, thoroughly exhausted by the fight. Jeremiah finds that he cannot give in to the apathetic norm of the status quo. He must remain involved in the will of God and strive for the good of his people, even though his own people have whipped and humiliated him.

The pressing question is, Where is that fire in the Black Christian community today? Jeremiah is our prophet also.

Where Is the Fire?

Where is the prophetic rage over our own behavior and practices within our community? Where is the outrage over the barriers of racism that still exist and by all counts are not dissipating but growing stronger in this country? Is there a deep-seated concern for the plight of our people, the majority of whom live in or near the national poverty line? Is there anything about us, our story, our history, that we hold sacred and will not compromise or sell off? Do we even wrestle with the risk of speaking out when we see or experience injustice, or are we silent partners in perpetuating unjust and racially skewed anti-Black business practices?

Does anything make us lie awake at night? Do we ask any more about whether we are gaining the world and selling our souls? Are we (especially the middleclass and upperclass Black Christian folk) fired up about anything? As Christians, is there anything consuming, explosive, pungent smelling or heated about our faith?

Ellis Cose in his book *Rage of the Privileged Class* documents the daily encounters that even successful middleclass and upper middleclass Blacks experience. Other writers have followed in his footsteps in later books. There is a difference between the rage Cose speaks of and prophetic rage. What Cose documents is a personal anger over personal hurts. Jeremiah's hurt is much broader. He weeps and is in turmoil for the hurt of his people. We as Black Christians are called beyond our individualistic outlook and the individualistic faith that is now so heavily promoted in evangelical circles.

Where is the fire of concern for our people? It is the rage of Jeremiah that is missing in our walk as Black Christians. Our image of fire is puny and trivial; consequently, so is our righteous indignation and our righteousness. We are more noted for going along to get along than for assaulting apathy. There is a status quo to our faith that did not exist for Jeremiah. Despite his best efforts to suppress it, the message he is commissioned to proclaim must come forth, and he is weary and worn out trying to stifle it within himself. Is there anything about our faith and concern for our people that pushes past personal hurts and will make us set aside or overlook our ego scars?

The standard reply is that we have a concern for souls, or that we have a concern for all people. Jesus never told us to save souls. He said make disciples. Furthermore, when have you run into a disembodied soul? Our Christology, what we proclaim about Christ, is about an incarnation. In order for God to get the message to us, he took a risk and became one of us, Emmanuel – God with us. He came in physical form. He was fully human, not a shell or a pretend casing: fully human.

To be concerned about everyone is to be concerned about no one. If no one is assigned to a task it never gets done. If there is not a concrete focus to our actions and our faith walk, it does not exist. Faith without works is dead!

What is the message that Jeremiah could not help but proclaim? It is the same one that got him into trouble in the first place. He has been given a message of judgment. He proclaimed that God was not pleased with Israel's worship practices, which also meant their societal practices. Religious practice infused their entire social–economic system every day of the week, so religion and society could not be separated.

The destruction Jeremiah predicts is not of the soul of his people but the actual destruction of their community, their nation, and in fact their entire way of life. What moves him is not some vague concern for the state of their soul or whether they will get into heaven. The norms of their society have become so skewed from God's original intention that they are in danger of being removed from the land God gave them.

The lack of Jeremiah's sense of prophetic rage among us has been noted by other thinkers. In his essay "The Crisis of Black Leadership" Cornell West describes the root of our ineffective political leadership.

> *What stood out most strikingly about Malcolm X, Martin Luther King, Jr., Ella Baker, and Fannie Lou Hamer was that they were almost always visibly upset about the condition of Black America. When one saw them speak or heard their voices, they projected on a gut level that the Black situation was urgent, in need of immediate attention. One even gets the impression that their own stability*

and sanity rested on how soon the Black pre-dicament could be improved. Malcolm, Martin, Ella, and Fannie were angry about the state of Black America, and this anger fueled their bold defiance.[12]

West calls it anger, but clearly it is the prophetic rage, the fire of Jeremiah, that West is describing. A colleague of mine agreed with this analysis but pushed one step further. If the fire does not exist in the congregation, then why have the clergy not stirred it up? West is also helpful here.

In stark contrast, most present-day Black political leaders appear too hungry for status to be angry, too eager for acceptance to be bold, too self-invested in advancement to be defiant. And when they do drop their masks and try to get mad (usually in the presence of Black audiences), their bold rhetoric is more performance than personal, more play-acting than heartfelt. Malcolm, Martin, Ella, and Fannie made sense of the black plight and powerful manner, whereas most contemporary Black political leaders' oratory appeals to Black people's sense of the sentimental and sensational.[13]

Where Is the Fire?

Cornell West does not address the crisis of Black clergy leadership, which is wise since he is not clergy and familiar with our ways, but I am a preacher so I can say it. There is a crisis in Black clergy leadership. West's analysis of Black political leadership can readily be transferred to Black clerical leadership.

There is no fire like Jeremiah's in the Black Church. The state of Black America concerns few of us to the point of prophetic rage. At times, our rhetoric is fiery, but that is mere play-acting. We are not upset unless the act is so egregious and media–hyped that it becomes safe to be outraged. Even then we treat the symptom and never keep our attention focused long enough to root out the disease.

Two things must be recognized here. First, the Black Church, contrary to popular myth, has always contained only a small minority who were concerned about the state of Black America, our community, and our people. We have a long history of accommodation to the status quo and existed for many years by mouthing the twin mottos, "Go slow" and "We will be rewarded by and by."

Secondly, a prophetic rage does not mean that we act without thinking or planning. Quite the contrary, if there is real fire, real prophetic rage, especially in this environment, strategic thinking, planning, and implementation are demanded if we are really going to make a difference.

Jeremiah wrote down his proclamations, and when his writings were destroyed, he wrote them again. A prophetic rage brings a tenacity and persistence. It is not a lighter–fluid fire that flames up quickly and just as quickly is out. Prophetic rage is like the white-hot coals of a cooking fire. The coals take longer to heat. The flames are small and the fire compact, but the heat is intense and will last for hours. This kind of prophetic fire will sustain us in doing the mundane, unexciting follow–through that is vital for significant and sustainable change.

Where is the fire in our clerical leadership? Where is the gut–level concern and the dynamic tension that are revealed in a true concern for Black people? There is little evidence that fiery concern exists.

We hold conference after conference on church growth, evangelism, preaching, worship, and music. There are none on the state of Black America and the people of the Diaspora. We have a crisis. I have sat on many ordination councils and taught many classes of prospective clergy and must sadly conclude that many simply lack the desire to do the critical analysis necessary for Black Christians to do effective work. Some of our clergy leadership are simply lazy and unwilling to break a sweat for anything except a bigger edifice, a luxury car, or the latest fashion.

Our church growth is measured by quantity, not quality. Our voter registration is focused on numbers registered, with little regard for becoming part of the political process, mastering the game of politics, holding our poli-

Where Is the Fire?

ticians accountable, and demanding a piece of the pie vs. gratitude for cast–off crumbs. The advent of more women clergy has changed the focus somewhat, but sadly, in too many instances it is more of the same. The Full Gospel movement has a focus solely on worship and what takes place on Sunday morning. Little or nothing is preached, taught, or done about the grinding injustice that is killing our people. The fire is sorely missing.

These are harsh words, I know. But if we are to do anything about our situation here in America and really be advocates for Africa and for our brothers and sisters scattered over this hemisphere, we must first recognize the gravity of the state of our faith. The kingdom of this world will never become the kingdom of God unless we do get some fire shut up in our bones.

While I recognize that there has been improvement in the state of Black America and things are different from the Civil Rights era, to use a biblical metaphor, we have only crossed the Red Sea. There is a wilderness yet to cross and a promised land to conquer. We have not arrived yet. Jesus said, *Whatever you ask in My name, I will give it.* I wonder if we will have the courage to ask God for a prophetic raging fire in our bones.

Arm me with jealous care,

As in thy sight to live,

And O thy servant Lord prepare

A strict account to give.

FOR SUCH A TIME AS THIS

Do not think that in the king's palace you will escape any more than all the other Jews. For if you keep silence at such a time as this, relief and deliverance will rise for the Jews from another quarter, but you and your family will perish. Who knows? Perhaps you have come to royal dignity for just such a time as this.

Esther 4: 13b-14

These, the opening years of the 21st century, have fallen far short of the predictions of paid pundits and our own hopes. Fifty years ago it was thought this century would be the age of space travel. Our cities would contain clean if not antiseptic streets and minimalist buildings. Our only worry would be what to do with all the leisure time afforded us by modern conveniences. On the dark side, we might be concerned about what to do with the workers who were no longer needed.

During the turmoil of the 1960s, we had hoped that in the 21st century equality would reign and perhaps collective and individual judgment would be based on character, not color. Integration would bring benefits to all, as we learned that harmonious living between races is indeed possible. Poverty would be defeated and hunger and ill health would be on their way out. As we grew closer, our vision got smaller, but we were still positive.

Capitalism was victorious as the Eastern bloc nations fell and the Soviet Union split apart. America was the only reigning superpower left. We would enter the 21st century as the leading economic system in the world, having thoroughly defeated the Japanese management practices that had caused us such hand ringing in the 1980s.

America's superior technological prowess and investment acumen resulted in a multibillion-dollar surplus and a bullish peacetime expansion, the longest on record. Why, even Black folk had to simply believe, work hard, invest, and the bountiful blessings of finance would flow. Democracy was great. Our vision was smaller, but still, progress was being made.

Then the 21st century began in reality. As I write, in the summer of 2004, America has no large vision. What vision there was has shrunk. This should be no surprise. There were indicators early on that we as a nation were losing our ability to focus on big ideas and a large vision. As the century opened, we spent months and millions focused on semen stains and the genital shenanigans of our Chief of State. Our democratic system was focused for two months on dimpled and hanging chads. We went from one small thing to another. Above all, our most prestigious court made a split decision that installed a president and indelibly stamped disappointment on our age. Allies and foes compared this nation to the "banana republics" we had disparagingly regarded in our foreign policy.

On September 11, 2001, the last remaining superpower was attacked and wounded, but that was not the worst of it. Modern America has crossed over into unfamiliar terrain as a nation. Fear hovers overhead. Fear of the worst is the backdrop of our politics, our businesses, and our lives. A check over the shoulder, a watching of our step, a glance of uneasiness is becoming habitual in our national life.

This nation has entered the life of the "less than." We are now the ones who can at any time be struck and laid low. We are now the ones who are on the receiving end of random violence. There are no distinguishing characteristics that divide the deserving from the undeserving, the good from the not so good and the truly bad.

When we live with a "less than" mindset, individual and human distinctiveness is lost. Individuals are placed in one homogenous category, "Americans." This labels us as group property. So many chairs, tables, lamps, and "Americans" were destroyed in yesterday's terrorist attack. There is a coldness and detachment in this process. People are reduced to a psychic subhuman level. We have seen this phenomenon before and already have a label for it: America has become "niggerized."

Meanwhile, back at the ranch, literally, Jr. has squandered the surplus, the boom has busted, and we are in a war started for questionable reasons in a preemptive manner that is unprecedented in America's foreign policy. War rhetoric and terrorist threat levels regularly divert us from the necessary assessment of our country, our leadership, and our vision.

The more important question is, What vision do we as Black folk now have at the beginning of the 21st century? Integration has not proved as beneficial as we had hoped. White folk have not proved as benevolent or as Christian as we believed. Lynching, police brutality, racial profiling, poverty, hunger, and ill health still torment the majority of our population. Add to that ill-fated mixture widespread obesity, AIDS/HIV, and homelessness and the warning bells for crisis ought to be ringing. At the very least, a general inquiry into the long-term implications of these problems as they affect the fate of our people needs to be undertaken.

We Blacks are Americans, and the events of the opening years of this century effect us also. However, any assessment of our condition as Black Americans must not forget the historic reality that whatever happens to the majority of this nation happens to us first and worst. All socioeconomic indicators confirm the proverb, "If White America gets a cold, we get pneumonia."

If being American now means living in fear, what does that mean for us "who have been there, done that." Ominously, it means in some instances that our issues become irrelevant because fear and self-preservation become the order of the day. Rights, minority concerns, diversity issues can be swept aside, for fear rules.

For Such a Time As This

On the other hand, there is opportunity, for we have an expertise of experience in succeeding despite fearful situations. However, success will not be ours until we look at our own community.

What is our vision of ourselves? Where do we want to go? Our vision is disappointing and for some it is a hearkening backward to an era, a dream, a few sentences of a 17–minute speech that spoke of little White children and Black children playing together and the creation of a place where we all can get along. Some have bastardized those few sentences and promote a "color blind society," which is only a veil for continuing the status quo. For others there is the hope of blending in so they can anonymously disappear into the mix. Others react by detailing the grand conspiracy, whose players change from month to month and nothing is ever completed. Nothing is ever done.

Let me put forward two underlying assumptions that I believe must form the foundation of our future. First, we need a goal as a people, not simply as Americans or Christians. One, being Black is not an option. Our history and contemporary reality make that a non-option. Black people are readily identifiable and cannot go slipping through society unnoticed.

Secondly, as Black Christians in the Western World we have a particular story to tell of deliverance and redemption. We cannot keep silent about what God has done for us. When we neglect to proclaim what God has done for us and through us, we forget God and slump into idolatry.

What is our vision? Do we have a collective goal? Sadly, as a people we have a muddled vision and our direction is unclear. We say we want opportunity, equality, equity, but those are vague terms that leave nothing to really push toward. In past times our goals were more definitive: freedom, the right to vote, and quality education. No longer are we debating tactics or strategy. We do not know where we are going or how to find our own place in society. We are wandering in circles.

This is a crisis, for a people cannot survive without purpose, direction, and a sense of mission. It is a quiet crisis characterized by malaise and an energetic misdirection. The malaise is the nihilism of hopelessness. The symptoms are drug use, alcoholism, and violence.

The energetic misdirection is evidenced by rampant, self-indulgent materialism. We seek the acquisition of things simply for status and pride rather than for necessity. It is a "he who has the most toys wins" mentality. It is the foundation for greed, excess, and luxurious leisure. When threatened with the loss of those toys, a fearful panic sets in that results in a betrayal of community consciousness and a defensiveness that strikes first and asks questions later. One's sole concern becomes: How am I doing? What am I losing? How can I preserve what I have? How can I continue my status as HNIC (Head Negro in Charge) or ONIC (Only Negro in Charge)?

These are the central concerns of our existence. This is a quiet crisis, yet it is a crisis nonetheless in a significant portion of Black America.

For Such a Time As This

What do we do in such a time as this? That is the question of the hour, and it comes from the Book of Esther. Esther, the noble heroine, is known primarily for her resolute declaration to her uncle Mordecai that she would go before the King and risk her life for her people, and "if I perish, I perish."

Esther's story was told to inspire all to emulate her faithful and prayerful ways. However, that is only a partial and cursory reading of the Esther saga. Key unexamined elements speak to our contemporary situation and are important to the charge we have to keep.

As Dr. Jeremiah Wright points out in his collection of sermons, Esther was not her real name. Her given name was Hadassah; Esther was her "passing" name. We do not talk about passing anymore, though it was the goal of the skin–color hierarchy we created among ourselves and it ruled much of our world until very, very recently.

> If you're light, you're right
> If you're brown, stick around
> If you're black, get back

That was our mantra from slavery until recent years. On second thought, maybe it has not disappeared but gone underground and wormed its way deeper into our unconscious. There are a lot more Black blondes now than in the early days of *Ebony* and the fashion revolution of the

1960s. How did various shades of blonde and red hair creep back into Black culture as a fashion statement? Was it simply a response to the minstrel-like antics of a professional basketball player who changed his hair color from game to game? Is it coincidental that it happened at a time when affirmative action was withering under assault, conservatism had taken firm hold in both sacred and secular American circles, and some political leaders strove not to be known as Black leaders? At this point, I simply raise questions.

Under instructions by her uncle Mordecai, Hadassah had hidden her identity and passed into Persian high society as Esther. She had blended in so well that she out Persianed the Persians. As queen, she was the poster girl of the beautiful people. Socially and politically she held the same views as the ruling elite.

Esther knew nothing of the genocidal decree against her own people until Mordecai (who was living outside the gated community) told her, and her initial response was to refuse to do anything on their behalf. Her sole concern was what she might lose and how she might preserve what she had. Esther was parked on that decision until Mordecai confronted and challenged her.

It is ironic that the story of Esther is so imbedded in our Black culture, so relevant to our situation, and remembered mostly for her final declaration. Yet the most salient point and the point most relevant to our times comes in Mordecai's challenge of liberation and empowerment.

For Such a Time As This

Liberation and empowerment never occur without confrontation and challenge. The words of Fredrick Douglas still ring true:

> If there is no struggle, there is no progress. Those who profess to favor freedom and yet deprecate agitation are men who want crops without plowing up the ground, they want rain without thunder and lightening. They want the ocean without the awful roar of its many waters. This struggle may be a moral one, or it may be a physical one, and it may be both moral and physical, but it must be a struggle. Power concedes nothing without demand. It never did and it never will.[14]

When Mordecai confronts Esther, he enters a moral struggle and challenge; however, it is important to note that Mordecai's struggle is first a self-confrontation. Esther's words confront him with his own sin. She became who she is by following his instructions. This is more than "being careful what you wish or pray for." This is "behold what you have created."

To paraphrase a comicstrip, we have met the enemy and she is us. Her mother birthed Hadassah; Mordecai birthed Esther. He does not like what she has become, but he cannot be too harsh. His hand is in it too deeply. Yet

the circumstances and situation of his people demand that
he challenge himself and his niece. His words must challenge, not kill. He cannot let himself deny his own culpa-
bility, or Esther hers. "Perhaps for such a time as this you
have come into the kingdom." This helps to focus the contemporary direction of the confrontation and challenge for
us as Black Christians.

The Challenge

The challenge begins with a self-challenge. It requires
a candid look at who we have become.

Growing up in the 1960s, one of the general admoni-
tions in our community was, "Get an education. They can't
take that away from you." Although I am not sure, I suspect that this was prevalent elsewhere besides Northern
urban communities. Churches responded by creating scholarship funds. I can remember clearly the special Sundays
when the high school and college graduates were the focus
of the service. Community organizations, fraternities, the
Masons, the Elks, all had their scholarship funds. There is
now an educated generation whose children are "getting an
education." We are the new Black middle and upperclass.
The challenge lies precisely at our feet.

We are the beneficiaries of Brown vs. Board of Education, the legislation of the civil rights era, and the GI Bill.
We are more than the talented tenth and what used to be

known as the Black bourgeoisie. Our ranks are broader and deeper. We hold at least a high school education. Whether teachers or CEOs, government workers or politicians, we hold significantly less economic clout than Whites in similar positions. We are also the group whose liberation role is ill-defined.

Forty percent of the African–American population is at or below the poverty line. These are the truly needy that even many anti-affirmative action opponents will concede need some sort of hand up. Scholarship funds exist just for this group if they can manage to get the right test score or GPA or sing, dance, catch, throw, etc. The old admonition and its defining liberation theme, "get an education," still rings true for this group.

However, we, the Black middle and upperclass, find ourselves in liberation limbo. There is no prescribed role for us. We exist like Esther, inside a gated community unaware of the crisis that exists among our own people. In a sense we are the crisis. Much hand wringing has been chronicled about the dearth of Black leadership. The missing Black leadership is not due to lack of education. It is because there is a lack of consciousness among those who possess the intellectual tools and wealth to make the structural changes needed for Black community empowerment. I am not talking about the consciousness–raising of the 1960s, which awakened Black pride. I am talking about the consciousness that comes from clearly seeing a goal and working toward it with all of the energy and creative awareness one can muster. It is the lack of a tangible goal and a misunderstanding of the role of our socio-economic, "got an education" group that is at the heart of our crisis.

Actually there is a general goal, an Esther goal: Out Persian the Persians. Once basic survival needs are met, our general goal appears to be "obtain the same material goods as others." Little is desired beyond maintaining the luxury lifestyle. It is precisely because no goal has been defined that these ranks, which should be providing the leadership, are in liberation limbo. Let me speak more of this role.

In the era of slavery there were free Blacks. Most were poor and eked out a living in Northern cities. There were a handful of such who managed to be successful enough to live beyond subsistence. David Ruggles, bookstore owner, Henry Highland Garnett, Presbyterian minister, Robert Purvis, lumber store owner, Charles Redmond, J.W.C. Pennington of New York, all were active in the abolition-ist movement and felt a duty to be deeply involved in the struggle for freedom. Later, the role was defined as being "a race man," a promoter of uplifting Black folk.

What role now? It has become fashionable to back away from Blackness and a firm commitment to Black empow-erment. Whether it is couched in the language of diversity or in the nondescript term "minority," there is an amor-phous vagueness that saps the strength from any pro-Black liberation argument. The question now is, Once we "have arrived" is it no longer relevant to assume a liberation role?

What is our agenda? For those who question our need for an agenda, I offer this reminder: America has a long anti-Black history, and we can never simply blend in and not be noticed by White society.

In short, I contend that we are like Esther who has forgotten her Hadassah identity and is happily and busily ensconced in Persian life. Like Mordecai, my aim is to challenge, not denigrate. There is a crisis, and it is our crisis. Without serious Black leadership to strategize how to use all available resources of intellect, position, policy, and wealth to open doors of opportunity for Blacks, we will not be safe in the boardroom or behind the gates of social class.

Let me say more about the role of leadership. An example of the crisis upon us is the Million Man March, October 16, 1995. An outpouring of Black men flooded the Washington mall. It was said that no one could have called together that many persons but Louis Farrakhan. No civil rights leader, Christian minister, Black politician, or Black business owner or leader could have pulled off that feat, for no one had his ability to connect with the majority of Black men.

This was the largest gathering of African-American males in the history of this country. Participants spoke about what a great feeling it was. However, time has proven that that was all it was, a feeling. Sadly, beyond the stimulating moment, little of substance was produced. Minister Farrakhan spoke for more than an hour, but few can remember anything he said beyond some general comments about Black men assuming responsibility for themselves, their families, and their communities.

It spawned a string of imitations, including the Million Women's March, the Million Youth March, and the Million Family March, each weakening in effect. Finally, as in so many other cases, the majority culture appropriated the concept for themselves. White mothers held the Million Mom's March with similar results. Stimulation for the moment, but little else produced.

No sustainable organization—political, economic, or social—evolved from that Million Man March moment and no fund accountability. Of course, this is no different from the church conventions that are held annually. Much fanfare for the moment, little substance follows. Little impact is felt in our churches and communities. Politically, there is the same scenario. Each year the Congressional Black Caucus holds its convention. The fashion show is a highlight, and the brain trust meetings gather with little follow-up.

There is a consistency to our crisis. It is style over substance. In the 2004 presidential race, with all the Black elected officials available, only an activist/minister/social critic could make what at best can be called a symbolic run for the presidency of the United States. Much media hype, but little substance followed. To move beyond a symbolic run, a candidate must have enough experience in governing, politics, organizational management, and creating a broad base of support for effective, substantial change.

A new face, Barack Obama, a Democrat senator from Illinois, arrived on the political scene. Of African and Caucasian parentage, Obama made a tremendous speech at the Democratic National Convention that caused some commentators to gush that he could be the first African American president. Perhaps so, but we have always had someone who could speak well. The question remains, Will there be enough think tanks, experienced political operatives, and business leaders in the background to make a substantive run for an African American presidency a reality? Without such organizational structure, an African American candidate could only run on an agenda not of our making. The positive note is, at least at this writing, there has been no verbal disavowal of Blackness by Sharpton or Obama.

We do have a group of so-called new leaders who do not want to be identified as Black leaders. They want to be known simply as leaders. Question: can one be both a Black leader and a leader of others? The denial argument has two fallacies. First, once you are Black you are Black; you cannot change your race or ethnicity, and only a dysfunctional person would want to. Secondly, you can function in more than one capacity at the same time. I am the father of three daughters. Am I the father of one and not the other two? Can't I advocate for one and treat them differently? Can't I advocate for them differently, as they have different needs, and yet love them all. Of course I can, and we do. There is a disingenuousness in this claim to be "just a leader." It really is a sense of shame and distancing from one's people. Any real leader cannot disavow who they are, who God has made them, and carry the mantle of leadership for anyone.

These are but a few examples of our leadership crisis. So why am I challenging Black middleclass and upperclass Christians? Succinctly, we have come into the kingdom "for such a time as this."

We did not ask to come here as a people, but here we are. We were not meant to survive except as a workforce; we have been and are now more than day labor and subsistence farmers. We now have resources. Economically we are the richest poor folk in the world. The challenge is how to use these resources: *to whom much is given, much is required.* (Luke 12: 48b)

We are missing the mark in terms of true stewardship. We continue the phenomenon that Malcolm X noted in the 1960s. We pour our resources into church buildings and fail by and large to build businesses and the communal consciousness that would allow these businesses to thrive and our people to flourish as a community.

For Such a Time As This

This is not to say that there have not been attempts, but some very public missteps, exposing the greed and mismanagement of our leaders, has created a chasm in the public trust and credibility of some clergy leaders. The fiasco of the former president of the National Baptist Convention, Inc., the Rev. Henry Lyons and the collective work of the Revelation Corporation still cast a pall over our churches.

A review of these failures can be instructive, but I mention two contributing factors in the nature of our church organizations. One, we do not demand a collective financial accountability. Second, the leadership that is available in our corporate ranks and the ranks of the entrepreneurial Black community is largely absent from leadership in our church organizations. The leadership that Black folk need must be savvy, strategic, and committed.

Unlike the Esther story, one person cannot be the spokesperson for African American people or even the whole of Black Christendom. Leaders with various skill sets are needed to serve in organized groups of Spirit–filled, strategic thinkers and focus on the greater good of our people as given in the Gospel. As servants of God, we then become the embodiment of the priesthood of all believers.

Challenge, Risk, and Faith

This is a challenge of vision, purpose, and mission. This inquiry into the substance of our faith requires an assessment of our unique faith story as a Black Christian people. Mordecai presents a challenge for life that demands a prayerful, active response.

After her initial refusal, Esther makes a decision that puts her at great personal risk. To help her come to grips with this decision, she engages in collective prayer. Mordecai prays outside the gate with his group while Esther prays with her inner circle. Then she acts.

Prayer was not an escape or an end in itself. It was, as Harry Emerson Fosdick termed it, prayer as a battlefield. Esther prayed for the strength and courage to take the risk that had already been decided on. Before she bent her knees in prayer, Esther knew that the nature of the crisis that she and her people faced required intentionality and risk. The substantial core of her faith in God, justice, and goodness was going to be tested. She needed the courage to act and take the risk.

The crisis we face as a people also requires risk and intentionality. There is no argument among us about the need to "give back to our community." Our faith obligates us to give back. Part of the "give back" response often is to start a scholarship fund, feed the homeless, or volunteer at a nursing home for the elderly. While these are needed and noble, they are anemic reactions to the crisis we face at such a time as this. Moreover, they are far less than what we are called to do as disciples of Christ.

For Such a Time As This

There is no risk to starting a scholarship fund or undertaking similar activities. Any significant change in our condition is going to entail risk. As surely as Esther encountered risk, so must we. The essentials of our faith involve bearing a cross. There is no getting around it. The question is, Why have we settled on "giving back" and similar avenues of service as our sole response to the need of our people. I submit that it is because we have truncated vision and a limited sense of mission.

Mordecai's challenge to Esther is to expand her vision of responsibility and her mission and purpose. Until Mordecai confronts her, Esther's vision of responsibility is to her immediate family. She will take care of Mordecai and preserve her position so she can continue that care. Mordecai's challenge forces Esther to expand her vision of responsibility beyond the people immediately around her to those scattered in the various provinces of Persia.

Because this vision is so large, it means a risk of going before the king not once, but three times. Each time she risks dismissal and loss of her position as queen. Her mission is incomplete if she stops at any point short of her third entreaty. One can extrapolate the broadness of Esther's vision by her actions and the risk she is willing to undertake.

If we are to extrapolate the vision of middle/upperclass Black Christians by the actions we take when we "give

81

back," then that vision is exceedingly small. At most, that vision sees us as people with equal access to education. This is nice and palatable, but there is no risk. It is hard to politically fight or morally challenge the appropriateness of this small vision. Hence compassionate conservatism can embrace "leaving no child behind."

However, a vision of a Black community that is competitive socially and economically, just as any other ethnic community in America, is a much larger vision. A Black community that is able to be an effective advocate for other communities of the African Diaspora while seeing to it that some of the vast wealth of this country is distributed to them as a priority and not as an afterthought is a much larger vision. Using our positions of privilege to manifest this vision in reality is a much higher goal, and it involves risk.

Working toward a socially and economically competitive global Black community is risky business. Additional competition is not the desire of any organization and is at the root of the discriminatory and racist polices that have existed and continue to exist. A powerful African Diaspora is the vision White America fears the most. The majority of the lynchings that were carried out were not because of purported insults, as in the case of Emmett Till. The principal victims were those Blacks who were trying to start businesses in competition with Whites. The only domestic bombing carried out by a state government took place

For Such a Time As This

in Tulsa, Oklahoma, June 21, 1921, when Black Wall Street was destroyed.

For our community to embrace this vision means we no longer are mere consumers, but competitors. This vision involves risk because to compete we must fight and wisely pick which fights to engage in immediately and which to delay. It involves risk because we must expose a pro-Black consciousness in a society that sees pro-Black as anti-White, anti-Hispanic, even anti-American, which is as ridiculous as saying because I love my family I am anti every other family.

This broad vision involves intentionality, and that always leads to an internal struggle and living in some discomfort. We must confess that we love comfort. Purposeful activity is always difficult, yet there is no real life without it. It is what is needed at such a time as this.

Most importantly, the vision has to do with our faith. To claim this sort of vision is to claim that God operates on our behalf in a unique way. It is to validate Joseph's claim to his brothers and sisters of the enslaving culture: "you meant it for evil, but God meant it for good." It is not bearing malice, but instead it is a proud proclamation of our unique, sacred history. God's love of us disavows shame and fear of our past and welcomes an active walk with Him.

We must step into our own, fight for our own, and advocate for our own people with prayerful resolve so that we may become instructive and inspirational to others, even as Esther did in her leap of faith. Nothing else will do for such a time as this.

NO CHEAP GRACE

In the fifteenth year of the reign of Emperor Tiberius, when Pontius Pilate was governor of Judea, and Herod was ruler of Galilee, and his brother Philip ruler of the region of Ituraea and Trachonitis, and Lysanias ruler of Abilene, during the high priesthood of Annas and Caiaphas, Word of God came to John son of Zechariah in the wilderness. He went into all the region around the Jordan, proclaiming a baptism of repentance for the forgiveness of sins, as it is written in the book of the words of the prophet Isaiah, "The voice of one crying out in the wilderness: 'Prepare the way of the Lord, make his paths straight. Every valley shall be filled, and every mountain and hill shall be made low, and the crooked shall be made straight, and the rough ways made smooth; and all flesh shall see the salvation of God.'"

John said to the crowds that came out to be baptized by him, "You brood of vipers! Who warned you to flee from the wrath to come? Bear fruits worthy of repentance. Do not begin to say to yourselves, 'We have Abraham as our ancestor'; for I tell you, God is able from these stones to raise up children to Abraham. Even now the ax is lying at the root of the trees; every tree therefore that does not bear good fruit is cut down and thrown into the fire."

And the crowds asked him, "What then should we do?" In reply he said to them, "Whoever has two coats must share with anyone who has none; and whoever has food must do likewise." Even tax collectors came to be baptized, and they asked him, "Teacher, what should we do?" He said to them, "Collect no more than the amount prescribed for you." Soldiers also asked him, "And we, what should we do?" He said to them, "Do not extort money from anyone by threats or false accusation, and be satisfied with your wages."

As the people were filled with expectation, and all were questioning in their hearts concerning John, whether he might be the Messiah, John answered all of them by saying, "I baptize you with water; but one who is more powerful than I is coming; I am not worthy to untie the thong of his sandals. He

will baptize you with the Holy Spirit and fire.
His winnowing fork is in His hand, to clear
his threshing floor and to gather the wheat
into his granary; but the chaff He will burn
with unquenchable fire. "

Luke 3: 1-17 NRSV

If we are to challenge the accepted and traditional interpretations of Scripture that Black people of faith have been taught, we must examine what might be called the ultimate act of stewardship: judgment of what we have done with the time, talent, and resources God has put at our disposal. We delve here into what is known in theology as eschatology – the science and thoughts of last things, the end of the world, death and final judgment.

Our faith does not stop at death; indeed it begins there. The Resurrection is central. No Easter is complete without the proclamation that Jesus got up early Sunday morning with all power in his hand. This is more than a point of preaching. The Resurrection, our hope and vision for the future, is central to how we live in our present age. Gayraud Wilmore in his book *Last Things First* makes the point "that what Christians believe about 'last things' may be first in terms of influence upon their behavior in the world."[15] We certainly cannot talk about reinterpreting texts without examining "last things."

Often heard in the spirituals are references of going to heaven. Eugene Genovese quotes an ex-slave, Annie Bell:

"Does I believe in 'ligion? What else good for colored folks? I ask you if dere ain't a heaven, what's colored folks got to look forward to? They can't git any where down here..."[16]

From the spirituals to Martin Luther King's "I have a dream" speech, there has always been some articulated vision of the eschatological future that is integral to the living out of our faith and heavily influencing our world. It is particularly malicious that the concluding words of hope in King's "I have a dream" speech ("judgment not by the color of our skin, but the content of our character") have been corrupted and redefined by Whites into the catch phrase "color blind society" and used as a blunt instrument to beat back any concessions to racial affirmation. We must reclaim, redefine, and reexamine King's hopeful vision for the future to guide our behavior, policy, and politics in this present age.

The starting point is not "where the lion lies down with the lamb" or the "peaceable kingdom" or that "crystal city whose streets are paved with gold." Rather, let us begin with the powerful heralding words of John the Baptist: *Prepare the way of the Lord*, as recorded in Luke 3: 1-17.

The text though familiar to most Christians is often overlooked in its significance to our faith walk. The role of John the Baptist, though prominent at the beginning of all four Gospels, is given short shrift in our popular theology. (This is ironic, given that at one time most Black people belonged to some branch of the Baptist denomination.)

No Cheap Grace

It is quite clear that John the Baptist understood that his role, at the very least, was one of a forerunner. His position was like that of the Old Testament prophet proclaiming the coming action of God. Indeed, he is identified with the verses of Isaiah 40: 3 *Prepare the way of the Lord.*

Yet for some reason we have failed to hear these words as a call to personal or collective action. At best, this call of John is generally interpreted as a "spiritual" call to get ready for God to act. Therefore, prayer and fasting are the appropriate responses to this text. This consistent misinterpretation has had some interesting reverberations in terms of social behavior. One of the most debilitating is the "victim mentality."

Now I am trespassing on the ideological territory of Black conservatives. Social critics such as Thomas Sowell, Ward Connelly, Armstrong Williams, Shelby Steele, and John McWhorter have discussed the victim consciousness that exists among us. In broad terms their argument is that we consistently see ourselves as victims of racism and, therefore, passively engage in and accept inappropriate and self-debilitating behaviors. Rather than taking responsibility for our own actions and our own circumstances, we blame our negative plight on racism.

Supported by an array of White conservative sponsors, these Black conservatives receive constant media attention; however, their arguments have generally not been well received in our community. There are many reasons for this. One is the failure of Black conservatives to acknowledge the structural inequities that have systematically denied us anything near a level playing ground in the competition of American economic life. Racism (when one group uses its disproportionate share of wealth and power to marginalize, exploit, exclude, and subordinate a weaker group) has historically targeted Black people. While not as visibly blatant as in the past, the structural inequities have been by no means dismantled and are still highly detrimental to Black economic, social, and political progress. We have not been simply victims; we have been and still are the central targets of systematic racism.

Secondly, Black pride and self-respect are lacking among Back conservatives. Far too much is made of the importance of acceptance. Cornell West in his essay "Demystifying Black Conservatism" notes,

> Most middle class blacks consistently supported the emergent black political class – the black officials elected at the national, state and local levels – primarily to ensure black upward social mobility. But a few began to feel uncomfortable about how their white middle class peers viewed them. Mobility by means of affirmative action breeds tenuous self-respect and questionable peer acceptance for middle class blacks... The importance of this quest for middle class respectability based on merit rather than

No Cheap Grace

politics cannot be overestimated in the new
black conservatism. The need of black conservatives to gain the respect of their white
peers deeply shapes certain elements of their
conservatism.[18]

Black conservatives promote the idea that until affirmative action came along, Blacks did not merit (earn) any
social benefits, although we labored to build this country.
They conveniently ignore the history of Black achievement
in scientific research and patents received, business, and
other arenas. They also ignore the destruction of Black
communities through lynching and other means.

Black conservatives do not acknowledge the massive
literacy rate achievement of Blacks. Under the poorest of
educational conditions illiteracy decreased form 98 percent in the mid-1860s to 40 percent by 1900 to 20 percent
by 1920.[19] Black illiteracy declined twice as fast as it did
for European immigrants who had access to much better
educational resources.

A profound sense of shame and second–class consciousness pervades the writings of Black conservatives.
There is the false assumption that Whites got where they
are by merit and that whites are more than willing to be-
stow ample rewards on those who prove themselves worthy. Where this assumption comes from is beyond reason.
Nothing in the acts of American society past or present
suggests that this sentiment is widely held or acted upon.

A CHALLENGE TO THE BLACK CHURCH

All of the Black conservative writers whose views are being heartily promoted by their sponsors are beneficiaries of affirmative action. John McWhorter in a column in *The Washington Post* is typical in his truncated views. In his concluding remarks in an op-ed piece he asserts, "It is up to the Supreme Court to bring out the best in all of us and outlaw the use of 'diversity' as a fig leaf for policies that have kept two generations of Black students from showing what they are made of."[20] In other words, over the last 20 years any Black student who benefited from admission to a school through affirmative action has somehow been denied the opportunity to truly excel.

McWhorter fails to acknowledge that affirmative action may have a hand in getting you in school, but it has little or nothing to do with whether you graduate. Our own catch phrase was "AA may get you in, but it won't get you out." Every day we had to prove ourselves with every professor.

McWhorter also states that he is in favor of affirmative action: "In a moral America, affirmative action in admissions must be based on socioeconomic class. In a nation riddled with inequality, we cannot require the same caliber of grades, scores, and advanced placement classes from students who have suffered true disadvantage."[21] He falsely assumes that Black students in the past who were denied access lacked the economic status to get in. According to McWhorter, economic status is the only true disadvantage.

No Cheap Grace

McWhorter falsely implies that any help for middleclass Whites has never been legislated nor given. It is this type of reasoning that relegates many of the writings of Black conservatives to the ash heap of propaganda.

Black conservatives refuse to acknowledge that Blacks have always been the primary targets of systematic racism. This blind eye and their lack of demonstrable Black pride cause most of us to suspect their motives as simply self-serving shills for deep–pocket sponsors.

So when Black conservatives do make an accurate judgment about our condition, it is easy to dismiss it. However, there is truth to the conservative diagnosis that there is a passive acceptance of inappropriate and self-debilitating behavior among our own people, which has resulted in Black folk not taking responsible and appropriate action to do all that we can to alter and better our circumstances. The conservatives call this behavior a "victim mentality."

Failure to take responsibility and passive acceptance of inappropriate behavior is not simply an affliction of African Americans. American culture is overflowing with evidence of this syndrome. From tobacco settlements to recent lawsuits blaming fast–food companies for obese children to the psychological pap of Dr. Phil and talk tabloid TV, there is ample evidence that this is also an American affliction.

However, the nature of this affliction in Black people is the central concern of Black conservatives and this author.

While the conservative solution seems to be, "Quit whining and get on with the hard work that you are unwilling to do and you will be rewarded on your merit," I am less optimistic about merit rewards and more concerned about the accuracy of the diagnosis and the recommended antidote for this behavior that is so seriously detrimental to us as a people.

First, I reject the label "victim mentality." Victim has the connotation of randomness, as in "crime victim," where one is, for no overt reason, the object of an assault, robbery, or burglary. There is also an implied lack of personally directed malice. Therefore, we speak of a crime of opportunity or the victim being in the wrong place at the wrong time. The perpetrator is an abnormality, and the victim is deserving of sympathy—but not too much sympathy if the crime is not too egregious because it could happen to anyone.

Black people were and are not the victims of racism. *We were and are the targets of racism.* I mean this in the same sense as a military campaign, where an identified enemy is a target and therefore the object of a strategically planned, orchestrated assault. Racism is a systematic group effort to target another group. It is not random acts simply perpetrated on one individual in the wrong place at the wrong time. Black people have been the targets of a strategic campaign to deprive them of the fruits of their labor. Slavery, sharecropping, and segregation were planned practices, enforced with legislation to prevent specifically Black people from taking advantage of social, political, and economic opportunities.

Red–lining is a planned practice of denying Black people mortgages and other access to capital. "Driving while Black" was proven in the state of New Jersey to be a planned practice of state police troopers interfering with the travel rights of Black motorists. The federal election debacle of 2000 in the State of Florida was not a random act. There is more than sufficient evidence that this was planned by the highest election officials to have black votes discounted. There is not sufficient evidence of planned complacency by the media, but the media reaction was generally complacent and compliant to the ruling elite of this country.

These actions, planned and implemented with a full intention to do harm, limit, psychologically and physically impair, cannot easily be glossed over or dismissed in a cavalier fashion. Neither can it be ignored that racism, the systematic targeting of Black people to limit their opportunities, socially, politically, and most importantly economically, still is far too widespread. We can debate how widespread this planned practice is, but from hate crimes to voter disenfranchisement to medical care inadequacies to economic inequities there has been study after study conducted to document that racism is at work targeting Black people.

Let us look at the perpetrators and their targets: us. A consciously planned system of exploitation is going to take an equally consciously planned system of repentance, restitution, and reparation to undo it. Some inadequate steps have been taken, but much, much more must be done.

It is unrealistic to think that the system of racism will simply come grinding to a halt because it is the right thing to do. Many civil rights leaders still fail to understand that it will take more time than we desire and a more effective strategy than social integration for us to make progress in this country.

In the meantime, we have a responsibility to do all we can to alter our circumstances and move ourselves out of the center of the target. The Black conservatives are correct; we cannot blame others for our own failure to reject inappropriate and self-debilitating behavior among our own people. We have been socially passive. The root of this passivity is not in the embrace of liberal policies but in our acceptance of a flawed theology as exhibited by the popular misinterpretation of the text cited at the beginning of this chapter.

John the Baptist makes a clarion call to his people. *Prepare the way of the Lord.* There is an obvious implied "you" preceding the command. The "you" says that there is an imperative act that each of us must do. It is helpful to look at the history of the text. The original herald was the prophet Isaiah. He was speaking to an exiled people about the vision that had sustained them through 70 years of captivity. Their hope had been to one-day return to Jerusalem. Now it was about to happen, but Isaiah was making it clear that they had a part to play if God was to act. They must make the highway in the desert. Their hope for the future would not instantly happen. They would have to do a lot of work to assist in its unfolding.

We too must "make a straight path for the Lord." We are the actors. God will not do this *for* us and neither will others. Even in an attempt to over-spiritualize the text, it is clear that we must play our part if the power of God is to be evident in this world. There is nothing passive about this text or the call to the people of God.

What many would like us to believe is that the color blind society has instantly appeared and nothing more needs to be done to dismantle racism. Nonsense! Nothing appears instantly except in fairy tales. Everything requires labor. A color blind society deals with the perception human beings have of each other. Perceptions do not change without years of work and a gradual shifting of thought. The fact that pseudoscientific books on the genetic inferiority of Blacks are still being published and widely distributed in mainstream America indicates that we are far from anything resembling a color blind society. To operate as though a color blind society were already present is simply illogical thinking and genocidal in its consequences.

A CHALLENGE TO THE BLACK CHURCH

As a Black people of faith, conscious of the reality of the world in which we live, the message we need to hear is that active preparation is part of the salvation drama. Passivity is not. Preparation is proactive, acceptable behavior. Mere reactive response to critical moments is not acceptable behavior as a people of God. Without our proactive preparation, the divine answer to the problems cannot be fully appropriated. We are fabulous for singing and saying how God will make a way, but the relevant question is, Are we actively preparing the "highway in the desert" for Him to use?

The failure of Black Christians to see ourselves as actors in the divine drama has had a curious effect. It has given rise to anti-intellectualism in the practice of our faith. Granted, the words of ex-slave Annie Bell must be taken seriously. There was a time when we "colored folk" had little expectation for "gittin any where down here." That has changed, but not the popular theology we live.

The idea that God is the Chief Actor and we simply respond to his dictates has created in our collective consciousness a split between the mind and the heart a god capricious in his actions. Feeling His presence supercedes the knowledge of His presence and acting in faith that He will be with us. In other words, our religious practice over-emphasizes creating the appropriate conditions for feeling God's presence and under-emphasizes the collective mental, physical, and spiritual strategic planning and preparatory actions that we must do.

No Cheap Grace

Historically, the split between mind and heart has been a class struggle. Carter G. Woodson in his book *Miseducation of the Negro* noted the phenomenon in the 1930s. Those who did attain higher education would leave the primitive Black Church and assimilate into other denominations, thereby depriving the church of the much needed leadership skills and economic resources they had obtained. Also, higher-class status was accompanied by a disdain for the emotional part of spirituality.[22]

Today there is a more refined struggle. The influence of the Pentecostal movement is pronounced in all denominations, and the spirit is no longer shunned or thought distasteful. However, the acceptance of the intellect into the life of the church is still lacking and even seen as detrimental to "real faith." The emphasis is on the feel of the spirit rather than the transformation of the mind. Those who have attained college degrees no longer shun the Black Church and its fervent spirit; however, the intellectual skills acquired still are vastly under–utilized. Critical, effective, and creative social analysis and engagement are not solid parts of our faith practice. An unthinking fanciful belief is still equated with spirituality.

This is not simply a problem for Black people. The popularity of the book *The Prayer of Jabez* by Bruce Wilkinson is evidence that magical formulas that require no insight, no inner preparation, and no righteous action are simply part of popular Christian culture. However, given all that is at stake, Black people cannot continue to operate within a flawed theology.

A CHALLENGE TO THE BLACK CHURCH

Cheap Grace

We act on what we think and believe. If our thoughts about God and faith are flawed, our actions will be also. One of the chief areas in which we have flawed thinking is the area of forgiveness. We Black people often call ourselves a forgiving people. Forgiveness is high on our list of virtues and emphasized as one of the marks of being a disciple of Jesus. This is true, but our behavior does not reflect the biblical understanding of forgiveness. Our behavior is to smile and forget about all past actions the moment anyone comes with an apology or the slightest act of contrition. Note John's message as the crowds come out to him. *You brood of vipers! Who warned you to flee from the wrath to come?* Loosely translated that means "you bunch of poisonous snakes, who warned you to run from the judgment that is to come?"

John the Baptist offers no ready-made, wholesale forgiveness for those who have come to follow him. He requires real acts of repentance. His message is that we must act if God is to manifest himself in his fullness, and that these acts of repentance must precede forgiveness. There is no forgiveness offered right away. True repentance delivers us from cheap grace. Cheap grace requires neither acts of contrition, tangible change in living habits, or meditative transformation of assumptions, preconceptions, or personal prejudices. The requirement is to show your commitment to a new way of living. A true change of heart is indicated by a change in behavior. John is insistent that this is the preparation necessary for salvation and the reception of the Messiah.

While forgiveness is widely proclaimed as a virtue in the Christian community, acts of repentance have not received the same attention, and we Black Christians have been complacent in perpetuating this heresy. Words alone satisfy us, and while talk is cheap, true grace is not. Reparations for slavery have not gained much of a hearing in our pulpits. We are too ready to forgive and forget.

The detrimental nature of this argument can be more readily seen as we look at the South African Truth and Reconciliation Commission which looked to the United States for guidance in race relations. Inevitably, the Commission adopted the same misguided thinking. Confess with an apology but refuse to back up the confession with economic acts of contrition or reparation. As a result, Black suffering, hunger, disease, inferior education, prison, and other socioeconomic indicators have changed little in South Africa. A few Blacks have obtained a decent income, political office, and a minority stake in the economy, but Whites still own and control 99 percent of all the wealth and resources.

These conditions in South Africa are only a mirror of conditions here in the U.S.A. A few Blacks have made it with a few crumbs from the table. Most Blacks have not because acts of repentance and reparation have never been required. Grace is cheap for the privileged but costly for the unprivileged. What is shameful is that we have labeled this Christian love, and nothing is further from the truth. True Christian love will only be understood when penitent acts become part of our lived theology.

We cannot continue in our flawed theology of forgiveness without repentance. John the Baptist charges us to raise the difficult questions of repentance. If you want the benefits of salvation, then repent. Banish greed! Share your goods and resources! Shun violence! Show your repentant heart by sacrificial, tangible acts—and then forgiveness will come.

Like John the Baptist, I may seem harsh, but this charge of repentance is not presented with a mean spirit. Black people have been well meaning, but we have allowed hypocrisy to flourish and many of our own people to continue in unrequited suffering. The Gospel demands that we do better.

Lest you think this is not the Gospel, I remind you of the encounter of Jesus with the tax collector Zacchaeus, as told in Luke 19: 1-10. When Jesus came to eat with him, unprompted, Zacchaeus said, *Look, half of my possessions, Lord, I give to the poor; and if I have defrauded anyone of anything, I will pay back four times as much.* Only then does Jesus say, *Today salvation has come to this house.* The acts of repentance were necessary for Zacchaeus to experience the fullness of God's blessing.

No Cheap Grace

Acts of reparation and repentance are quite plain in John the Baptist's proclamation, yet it is also quite plain that we have avoided this text, which prompts the question Why? Why has this emphasis been ignored? Because it goes against our very human nature of quietly fitting in and becoming a part of the crowd; it ruffles feathers and we become unpopular. We may also fear the retaliation of those responsible for hurting us, especially those who have power and control.

The reality is that despite our best efforts to be nice and accepting, we Black people have been retaliated upon anyway. Despite our best efforts to assimilate and integrate, anti-Black sentiment in this country has grown in recent years. The 1980 election of Ronald Reagan marked the beginning of the new rise in anti-Black sentiment. This was consciously cultivated by Ronald Reagan. The planned 1980 run for the presidency was kicked off in Philadelphia, Mississippi, a small town known for only one thing: the brutal murder of civil rights workers Micheal Schwerner, Andy Goodman, and James Chaney. When the Reagan campaign announced "Morning in America," they were announcing "Night Time in Black America." The gushing, near deification of Reagan by commentators and generally by Whites throughout this country is evidence that this message was and is thoroughly embraced.

The rollback of affirmative action, the quick diversion of assets away from domestic issues, the continuing public policies that deny Blacks the opportunity for broadcast control are retaliatory acts and evidence that we are living in a changed climate. Our perpetuation of Cheap Grace has left us little resources to combat these sweeping actions. Consequently, we have found ourselves patching the safety net and supporting a system that disrespects us, disempowers us, and puts enormous pressure on us to compromise our true faith.

Accountability

Part of what has been lost in our discussion of last things and vision for the future is the idea of accountability at the judgment. The last verses of John the Baptist's message have been left dormant. Usually the message is interpreted as the announcement of the Messiah's coming and simply that. However, the figures used by John are ones that are very vivid. *He will baptize you with the Holy Spirit and with fire. His winnowing fork is in His hand.* The images are from Psalm 1, and they are very powerful. That which is not pleasing to God will not last, but be blown away or burned up.

Though stewardship and the tithe has become more mentionable as part of our faith, we have failed to include them in the conversation of judgment. The very idea that we will have to be accountable for the funds and other resources at our disposal is anathema to capitalism and our way of thinking. We simply do not think that we can miss the final blessing of God, or lose our salvation, by not using money correctly. "There is always forgiveness," is usually our justification pronouncement.

We are not saved by silver, 30 pieces or $30 billion. Judas lost his salvation by giving in to the clink of an easy payoff. When he had a change of heart and tried to hold the chief priests and Pharisees accountable, it was too late. The Innocent was executed, the plotters walked away, refusing to be held accountable, and Judas in despair killed himself by an overdose of hanging rope. Accountability has a limited window of opportunity, and when it closes one simply becomes a co-conspirator or at best a silent endorser of injustice.

Holding others accountable is not difficult. Like John the Baptist, Peter, James, John, Paul, and so many others, we must take a stand when we know something is wrong. Isn't it strange that we good Black Christians have no trouble holding poor Black folk accountable, but we have great difficulty holding White people accountable. Perhaps we are more fearful than faithful.

Our actions have eternal, not just immediate, consequences. That was John the Baptist's point. Preparation, repentance, accountability are fundamental to who we are as Christians and to our faith. We cannot cheapen grace. The kingdom will be delayed unnecessarily if we do. We hold more in our hands than we think. A story is told of two young boys who wanted to fool a wise man. So one put a bird in his hand and conspired with his friend. "We will ask the old man whether the bird is alive or dead. If he says dead, we will open our hands and it will fly away; if he says alive we will crush it. They approached the old man and asked their question. He said to them, "The answer is in your hands."

We have grave and great responsibility in our hands. The futures of our children and their children's children are in our hands.

FROM EVIL INTENTIONS TO THE
GOODNESS OF GOD

Realizing that their father was dead, Joseph's brothers said, "What if Joseph still bears a grudge against us and pays us back in full for all the wrong that we did to him?" So they approached Joseph saying, "Your father gave this instruction before he died, 'Say to Joseph: I beg you, forgive the crime of your brothers and the wrong they did in harming you.' Now therefore please forgive the crime of the servants of the God of your father." Joseph wept when they spoke to him. Then his brothers also wept, fell down before him and said, "We are your slaves." But Joseph said to them, "Do not be afraid! Am I in the place of God? Even though you intended to do harm to me, God intended it for good, in order to preserve a numerous people, as he is doing today. So have no fear; I myself will provide for you and your little ones."

Genesis 50: 15-21b

In his book *The Prophethood of Black Believers* J. D. Roberts notes "that the black religious protest tradition has been attracted to the Old Testament, particularly the Exodus account and the words of the prophets of social justice."[23] He further notes that Black preachers:

Had a different worldview from their oppressors and they honestly sought a word from God. Theirs was a liberating interpretation of the entire Bible. The exodus and the leadership of Moses stirred their imaginations and gave them hope of deliverance...the prophetic word of social justice and the healing, comforting word of the psalmist have a special place for the black believer's faith. People that suffer from racism, a systemic form of evil with institutional expression, need a message of deliverance.[24]

Roberts' assessment is accurate and cogent. Even those of our people with nominal faith, who bristle at the term "Black Christian," will acknowledge that historically we have had an affinity for the Exodus story and the hope of deliverance.

Roberts' statement is also a springboard to identifying and addressing the theological crisis that affects us, the results of which fuel the malaise in leadership and the pervading sense of hopelessness (nihilism) in our communities.

The Nature of the Crisis

While we fail to voice it, the influence of our churches is slowly ebbing (though some may question the word slowly). We have a larger unchurched secular Black population than we have ever had despite the rise of TV ministries, mega churches, and the Full Gospel and Pentecostal movements. The Black Church's influence is waning. I am not just talking about numbers of individuals who attend Sunday worship. More critically, I am talking about the waning influence in the world of ideas. One's perspective, way of seeing the world, processing and filtering information, and analyzing life, has become less and less influenced by the Black Church.

From Evil Intentions to the Goodness of God

Roberts is correct in his analysis that the worldview of the Black protest preacher is liberation. To take it a step further, the influence of this worldview reaches beyond the preacher and the church in the realm of ideas.

Liberation ideas, the ground of our hope, were part of the worldview that Black Christians held and lived by. As a God–given right and a divine goal, liberation influenced our political and social leadership and Black people in general. Freedom was the moral high ground that many stood upon, and its influence was wide. Among leaders, freedom was a quest. Among the masses, it burned bright as a hope.

Today, however, freedom is no longer a focus. Television, radio, and print media have presented other worldviews and massaged their message into our minds. This message does not challenge White ownership and control but instead dangles a brass ring of inclusiveness and hides the reality of exclusion of Black people in the world of power, wealth, and resources.

Tolerance has gained the moral high ground, and that is why Rodney King's words were trumpeted again and again: "Why can't we all get along." Tolerance never challenges nor addresses economic inequities, economic exploitation, or economically abusive situations. Tolerance is purely social and purely secular. It is a by-product of an integrationist perspective that viewed our struggle primarily in social terms. The integrationist economic view was limited to where and how we spend our money and never addressed how we make and keep our money.

There is no divine imperative embedded in tolerance. There is no push, no "oomph," no boldness, and no guts. Tolerance is apathy without the shrug of the shoulders. It is the lukewarmness indicated in Revelation 3:16. Tolerance is the equivalent of being "nice." Nice is never empowering. Evil will not give way to niceness, nor praise, nor speaking in tongues, nor praise dancers, nor step teams. But these worship practices are not the problem. Our problem is much greater and compounded by an emphasis on a spirituality that is non-sacrificial.

Spirituality is very popular. One only has to go to their local bookstore; many now have an entire section dedicated to "spirituality." Looking at the many devotional books published, one could conclude that there is a new-found spiritual seeking. However, most of these devotionals emphasize a spirituality of self-development, self-fulfillment, and achievement. Enlightenment and self-gratification become one and the same. I have written elsewhere about the emphasis on the individual versus the collective, but let me further expand upon those thoughts.

The elements of redemption and redemptive suffering have disappeared. The core of our faith is that the suffering of Christ was redemptive. His suffering upon the Cross was for a reason. By his stripes we are healed (Isaiah 53: 5). As our ancestors followed Him, their suffering was not in vain; and so too as we follow Him, our suffering will also be redemptive.

Thomas Shepard asks the right question about the responsibilities of discipleship in his well known hymn *Must*

From Evil Intentions to the Goodness of God

Jesus Bear the Cross Alone and All the World Go Free? His answer was of solid doctrine: "No there's a Cross for everyone and there's a Cross for me." What we have now is a different answer. The popular idea of individual spirituality has answered the question, "Must Jesus bear the Cross alone?" with a resounding "Yes!" We must follow our bliss, pamper our spirits, and satisfy our well–being. The last two Beatitudes have disappeared.

> *Blessed are those who are persecuted for righteousness' sake, for theirs is the kingdom of heaven.*
>
> *Blessed are you when people revile you and persecute you and utter all kinds of evil against you falsely on my account. Rejoice and be glad, for your reward is great in heaven, for in the same way they persecuted the prophets who were before you.*
>
> Matthew 5: 10-11

How did we arrive at this theological juncture, where one of the pillars of our Christian faith is severely weakened? More important is how do we move from this point to bring ourselves in line with the scriptures and basic Christian doctrine?

We solve our theological crisis by remembering the living God of history.

Let me explain. Theology is the reflection and consideration of what God has done. This reflection forms the basis on which we live our faith today and gives direction to our service and hope for the future. Our reflections and considerations rest on the foundation of Holy Scripture, for it is the biblical account of God's acts that define our understanding.

However, the interpretation of scripture is not the sole ground of our theological reflection. As we understand God's past acts, we interpret our own history and our own present. We ask, Is there any word from the Lord for this day and time? Our God is a living God, not confined to the pages of biblical history. He had a hand in our history and is present shaping our future.

It is this reflection that is uniquely the purview of the Church. Black Church leaders, pastors, scholars, and academicians have failed to adequately plum the depths of our sojourn in this hemisphere as a God-called people. We have a unique history, a salvation history, yet our uniqueness has been relegated to rhetorical flourish. Occasionally we refer to our unique history, usually during Black History Month, but seldom in the consistent manner of a people who truly see God's hand in their past.

Our people's salvation history is significant. In their Babylonian captivity the children of Israel asked, *How can we sing the Lord's song in a strange land?* (Psalm 137: 4). Black Christians can testify that we have learned to sing the Lord's song in a very strange land. No other people on earth have been displaced as we have or in the manner that we have. We need not regard our slave history as an era of shame. Slavery was a system of unprecedented physical and psychological cruelty and economic exploitation. The systematic degradation of a people left some indelible scars and some memories that are hard to erase and in most cases hard to speak about. Yet in the midst of this inhumane treatment, unlearned slaves raised some penetrating theological questions.

The words of a slave, Charlie Moses, need to be taken seriously.

O Lord! The way we niggers was treated was awful. Marster would beat, knock, kick, kill. He done everything he could 'cept eat us. We was worked to death. We worked all Sunday, all day, all night. He whipped us till some jus' lay down to die. It was a poor life. I knows it ain't right to have hate in the heart, but – God Almighty – it's hard to be forgivin' when I think of old man Rankin.

If one o' his niggers done something to displease him, which was mos' ever' day, he'd whip him till he'd mos' die, and then he'd kick him roun' in the dust. He'd even take his gun an', before the nigger had time to open his mouf, he'd jus' stan' there an' shoot him down.[25]

Memories like that caused most of our ancestors to keep silent. It was too hurtful to be vocal. But now we have passed through and can look back. Indeed, we must look back. The theological questions raised by Charlie Moses and others of our ancestors must be answered. What of forgiveness in the face of such vicious disregard for human life? What, if any, message is in such misery? Why such suffering? Is there any redemption in this suffering? How do we understand ourselves as God's people, having come through this awful time of slavery and its first cousin, Jim Crow?

The Black Church has failed to help us understand what God was doing during slavery. What word from the Lord do we have for the entire Christian family? These are some of the theological questions with which we must wrestle.

In fairness, Black theologians have fought to declare that Black Christians have a legitimate word. In his introduction to *Black Theology: A Documentary History,* volume II, James Cone notes: "Most theological observers did not expect Black liberation theology to still be around during the 1980s and 1990s, not to mention the year 2000...Blacks are expected to preach, to sing and dance, and to play basketball but not to do theology."[26]

White Christianity, or Eurocentric Christianity, contends that we have no word—not overtly, but by omission. Church history curriculums still make little if any note of the Black Church and its uniqueness. Christian theology curriculums usually lump the Black American church in with liberation theology in a brief reference. The Black Church is an easily forgettable blip as far as they are concerned, and commentators rarely refer to our culture in their biblical commentaries and interpretations. Therefore, it is easy for American Christians to urge us to dismiss our heritage, forget slavery, put it behind us. Unfortunately, too many of us have bought into this specious claim and nod our heads in virtual agreement. There is still much for us to wrestle with among ourselves, but I will not waste time on that argument. We must reflect on what God has done, our message, and our mission. We turn where we have always turned, to the Holy Scriptures. The Old Testament is our beginning point, and specifically the story of Joseph.

Joseph's story is one that parallels our own. Joseph is the younger son of Jacob, by his wife Rachel, and a member of an extended non-nuclear family. He has known the blessing and curse of being the favorite. He is readily identified by his ability and his apparel, a coat of special sleeves, or many colors. Like our African ancestors, Joseph was sold into slavery by jealous brothers.

Joseph becomes a stranger in a strange land. His labor creates wealth for his master. Rewarded at first, he is then thrown into prison on a trumped up rape charge. Joseph's story is all too familiar. Despite the obstacles and the treachery, by divine intervention Joseph rises to a position of power. He is in charge of the warehousing and distribution of food for the superpower of his day, the nation of Egypt.

Years later, when his brothers come to request food to survive, Joseph covertly confronts them, not as a slave but as a successful businessman. After a series of tests, Joseph reveals himself to his brothers and invites them and his father, Jacob, to come to Egypt. It is only after he reunites with a father he thought he had lost and a family who thought he was dead that Joseph can begin to understand how God's blessing outweighs the suffering he has experienced. His suffering then takes on redemptive value.

Secondly, Joseph's frank theological assessment, "You intended to do harm to me," states that the actions of his brothers were evil, not misguided, ignorant, or unintended.

The assessment of evil is not to be taken lightly and stands in contrast to good. The darkness and depth of the evil highlights the brightness of God's blessing. The blessing vastly overcomes the evil but does not ignore its presence nor deny its reality even though Joseph's suffering is long past.

Third, when Joseph recognizes the goodness of God, it motivates him to do good and take continued care of his brothers and their families. He sees it as part of his purpose in life. This becomes his mission.

Our Mission

Joseph's theology teaches us that it is necessary for our theology to evolve, taking present circumstances into account. This challenges the popular idea that there has been only one message of Christian practice since time immemorial. As our understanding of what God is doing or has done changes, so must the emphasis of the Gospel message and the nature of our practice. The theology of our slave ancestors emphasized some issues that are no longer applicable and vice versa. At this point in our sojourn, we need a change of emphasis. Not for change's sake but because we understand more and have arrived at a new point in time. Freedom has been achieved, Jim Crow defeated. We are out of the pit, and now we find ourselves gifted with privilege. Now what?

We must assess history as frankly as Joseph did. Slavery, its trade and practice, is evil. It is malicious, intentional, and appeals to the worst instincts of human greed.

From Evil Intentions to the Goodness of God

To acknowledge less than that is to ignore the spilled blood. To forget the travails of our ancestors, denigrates their memory and diminishes the greatness of God's blessing of liberation.

We cannot forget slavery. It was not a social misunderstanding or a mere era of history. The African slave trade was vast in its scope, monumental in its impact, and the defining reality for us as a people.

We cannot dismiss slavery as an event that simply occurred and that is that. An entire population shifted. Estimates range from 15 million to 60 million Africans were captured and taken into slavery.[27] Up to 50 percent died in transport.

In England alone annual revenue from the slave trade amounted to approximately $60 billion in today's dollars and catapulted England into the single most powerful nation in the world.[28]

We cannot allow slavery ever to be reduced to a social misunderstanding. It was an institution fraught with greed, violence, and sexual exploitation. With frankness and without malice, we must assess the institution of chattel slavery as evil. Europeans were not the only people to benefit from slavery. Arabs and our own African brothers and sisters profited.

Europeans could not survive in the African interior. They only collected those Africans who were brought from the interior to the coast by other Africans. The slave trade predates the 1400s. Prior to the Europeans and long after them, Arab slave trades plied a trade in Africans. They were not our friends.

A CHALLENGE TO THE BLACK CHURCH

It is easy to condemn the interlopers, but we must also grapple with the evil of Black-on-Black treachery. Without the complicity of our own, no transatlantic Diaspora would have occurred, certainly not in the vast numbers that it did. Black people have been hesitant to acknowledge that. Goree Island's doorway of no return was not constructed solely by European hands; greedy jealous Black hands were also involved.

Finally, in applying Joseph's theology, we must also acknowledge our current circumstances. African Americans are citizens of the most powerful nation on earth. We have the most privilege, opportunity, and access to wealth of any Black people on earth. We are the richest poor folk on earth, followed only by the Afro-Caribbeans. Privilege and opportunity for us was not the intent of our oppressors. When politicians glibly comment that African Americans simply came here on a different boat from European immigrants, they minimize the cruelty and continue the legacy of economic exploitation. We were brought here to be worked to death for the prosperity of others. Thanks to God's grace, we survived and thrived.

This is not the end of the story. When we see the depth of slavery's sin, we can appreciate the greatness of God's blessing. As Joseph finally realized his mission, so we too must realize our mission. We as Black Christians have a divine charge to keep.

Joseph's theology and Jesus' mandate to care for the least of the least and love one another meld to give Black Christians a special sense of mission, similar to Joseph's

From Evil Intentions to the Goodness of God

and unique in modern history. Our charge is to forgive our brothers and sisters, care for our scattered family, and diminish the detrimental effects of our Diaspora. Just as Joseph used his position and power to gather his family and care for them, so must we. Just as Jesus did not leave His mother uncared for at the Cross, before He died for others, He cared for her. We have the same charge; take care of one another. Having stated our charge and mission, let us examine this further so that it does not remain empty rhetoric.

If a mission is to be successful, it must follow a plan. Our mission must follow the blueprint outlined in scripture. Before the disciples were sent out into the world, they were instructed to wait in Jerusalem until they were empowered by the Holy Spirit and then be witnesses in Jerusalem, Judea (familiar territory), Samaria (close by), and then the rest of the earth (Acts 1: 8). They were to move out only after being empowered to do so. We are fabulous for reacting solely on our emotions and leaving an ineffective witness in our wake. We also have a tendency to want to save everyone and end up benefiting no one.

As African American Christians, we have the charge, but we are not ready to move out. We are disempowered. We are hindered by a lack of knowledge. We lack knowledge of the extent of the Diaspora.

Recently, a group of students came to worship with us at the Florida Avenue Baptist Church in Washington, DC. Though they looked like dark Africans or African Americans, they explained in Spanish that they were Afro-Colombians. They firmly rejected the idea of being Latino or Hispanic. They emphasized that their roots were African. They explained that every South American country had a very significant population of Blacks, some as high as 30 percent despite official undercounts.

I shared that most African Americans had no idea that such significant populations existed. The students' benefactor, a Nigerian, said that neither did most Africans. These students shared that they did not know much about African Americans and our story. They only knew what had been exported to them through select American television sitcoms and movies. They had come to the church to hear first–hand Gospel music.

Our liberation story is not known. Our salvation history has not been shared. Our brothers and sisters perish for lack of knowledge and will continue to perish until we realize the depth and breadth of our divine mission.

We are hindered and feeble in power because we lack the necessary financial resources to equip and support Black missionaries for the length of time needed to make a significant impact. Our churches and denominations are still only able to make token and very temporary efforts. This is not to say that there has been no impact, but in the face of the tremendous need of those we wish to serve, our resources are woefully inadequate.

This is not because money does not pass through our communities. African Americans alone have $700 plus billion annual consumer dollars, but we have failed to aggregate our wealth. We are the richest poor folk in the world because our wealth is scattered. This is not by accident but by design. Wealth is not gathered or maintained by us.

From Evil Intentions to the Goodness of God

Financial advisors say that we do not save enough and make unwise investments. That is only partially accurate. A larger picture is necessary for us to take corrective action. We have lacked the inherited wealth, and access to capital that every other group has had to enable them to improve their financial condition. Since slavery, there has been a systematic effort to deny Blacks access to capital and the fruits of their labor. Though this effort has been blunted somewhat in the last 50 years, in large part, institutional financial racism continues to exist.

When we acquire capital, we have the "Black tax" to contend with—higher interest rates on mortgages and other loans, higher rents, and shoddy merchandise in stores not owned by us. Daily expenses negatively impact on our ability to accumulate disposable income.

However, our contemporary financial context is most affected by our own spending habits. In order for a community to thrive economically, a dollar must change hands eight to ten times within businesses in the community before it is spent outside the community. In Black communities the dollar changes hands once. In other ethnic communities people buy from their own, produce their own, and their dollars bounce as many as 17 times before they are spent outside of the community.

To better understand this phenomenon, I strongly recommend Dr. Claud Anderson's two works, *Black Labor/White Wealth* and its sequel *PowerNomics*. These are must readings.

Black people, we must get our economic house in order. We must change our inappropriate financial behavior to new group economics, for we cannot carry out our divine mandate without proper finances and knowledge. Whites, Latinos, Asians, Jews, and Arabs have not shared their financial knowledge because they have been the beneficiaries of our financial disarray. One only has to look at the various shops and business owners that have moved through our neighborhoods. In my home neighborhood, one local convenience store was owned by Whites, then immigrant Jews, and then Asians.

We must change our chaotic economic practices, which means we must adopt Joseph's mindset. Chattel slavery was meant for evil, but God intended for us to take advantage of every opportunity this country affords us politically, financially, socially, and spiritually. Then we will be the instruments of His peace and bring deliverance to the scattered sheep of Africa.

This means a new way of thinking. Black Christians have fallen prey to the gather and hoard mentality of unsanctified capitalism. We acquire for ourselves and give back only a pittance. Most damnable are the mega–ministries that flaunt extravagance in worship facilities, large pastoral entourages, automobiles, houses, and even private jets.

Joseph's theology has a different orientation. Resources are to be used for more than self-indulgence. However, the Black middle and upper-classes must first confess and avoid the sin of self-indulgence. Others must confess and avoid the sin of covetousness, which is the "trinket syndrome": when we get a little above our immediate need, we squander our meager funds on the latest gadget, fashion trend, or consumer product simply for appearance's sake.

From Evil Intentions to the Goodness of God

Why this emphasis on the Black middle and upper-classes? This is not to exempt others, but to whom much is given much is required. Slaves, poor people, the homeless, and the indigent are severely limited in their ability to help others. Middle and upperclass Black Christians have the resources, education, ability, and mandate to advocate for our people. The poorest and most distressed people of the world are the darkest. They cannot advocate for themselves.

Middle and upperclass Black Christians have the most disposable income and time needed to focus on the charge we must keep. We have been well positioned to exert our influence. The janitor who cleans the halls of Congress may be as intelligent as the congressional representative or staff member, but that janitor does not have access to power and influence as do members of the Congressional Black Caucus.

However, this does not mean that we simply wait for the superstar elite to lead the way. In the poignant parable of the talents, the successful servants were commended not for the amount of talents they had or the amount they acquired but for using what they did have. One servant was condemned not for what he lacked but for burying his talents in the ground and not making use of what the king had given him.

We have a golden opportunity to use what we have. There are many more opportunities and actions we can take to fulfill our mission as God's sun-kissed people. The bottom line is that we all have a part to play in turning what was meant for evil into God's good work for the life and well–being of our people. The blood, sweat, and tears of our ancestors still cry out. We all have a charge to keep.

Help me to watch and pray,

And still on Thee rely

O let me not my trust betray,

But press to realms on high.

THE VOW WE MAKE

I got a robe, you got a robe
All o' God's chillun got a robe
When I get to heab'n I'm goin' to put on my robe,
I'm goin' to shout all ov-ah God's Heab'n
Heab'n, Heab'n,
Everybody talking 'bout heab'n ain't goin' dere;
Heab'n, Heab'n
I'm goin' to shoud all ov-ah God's Heab'n

Additional verses
I got-a wings, you got-a wings
I got a harp, you got a harp
I got shoes, you got shoes

Negro spiritual

Our Father who art in heaven
Hallowed be thy name.
Thy Kingdom come
Thy will be done
On earth as it is in heaven.

Matthew 6: 9b-11 RSV

We cannot end these essays without examining heaven,
the most prominent image in our Black theology. The old

spiritual quoted above offers us some insight into what heaven represents to Black folk.

With its robes, wings, harp, and the living presence of God, heaven is a much different place from our present inhabitable world. There is an exclusivity about heaven: "everybody talkin' 'bout heab'n ain't goin' dere." Entry is not automatic, and the mere profession of one's Christianity does not guarantee a place in heaven. Note that the world situation of the singers is woven into the vision of heaven. These slaves knew too many "Christian" slave owners who talked one way but were "mean as the devil." They themselves could not do much about it, but they were confident a just God would not be fooled by Whites' hypocrisy.

There is concreteness about heaven and the final reward. "All God's chillun got shoes." It is clear that shoes is not part of their world, and they were firm in their conviction that everyone deserved a pair of shoes. This might seem to be a quaint touch or somewhat unenlightened, but these slaves made a profound connection. The kingdom of heaven is a reality very much connected to the everyday reality of their world. It is precisely this connection we need to revisit in our thinking by revisiting the Lord's Prayer, which we recite by rote and mindlessly sing Sunday after Sunday. At the center of the prayer that Jesus taught, is the kingdom of heaven.

Thy kingdom come, thy will be done on earth as it is in heaven. This is an arresting phrase, for if we examine the Gospels, we find that the kingdom of God, or the kingdom of heaven, is a central image in the preaching of Jesus. The Gospels present over 50 kingdom sayings. Jesus spoke of the kingdom of God as being both present and future. In Matthew 4 :17 Jesus proclaims *"Repent, for the kingdom of heaven has come near."* Luke 4:17 states *"the kingdom of God is among you."* Also, *"My kingdom is not of this world"* (John 18: 13).

We will not try to resolve the seeming contradictions but note that the kingdom was central to the preaching of Jesus. The kingdom could be entered into by repentance and participating in its divine presence. It is quite clear that though our orientation toward the kingdom is the future, it is not solely in the future. There is a present–day characteristic, for the kingdom is growing and one must be prepared for its arrival.

However, this does not mean that we simply wait for the kingdom to drop from heaven intact or that the ethical nature of the kingdom is to become manifest only after we die. The kingdom of God is upon us *now*. That is what we pray and work toward, but the concept of the kingdom of God continues to remain fuzzy. We think that the kingdom is located somewhere over proverbial Jordan. Also our understanding of the kingdom comes from song or the climax of the sermon and not from scripture.

For example, when I first asked a Wednesday night Bible study class what the kingdom of God was like, the answers were quite typical:

"Every day will be Sunday."
"We will have golden slippers and long white robes."
"The wicked will cease from troubling and the weary will find rest."
"The lion will lie down with the lamb."

While these responses are not without biblical reference, there was an inability to describe the kingdom of God in contemporary terms. Though we pray about and work toward the kingdom of heaven, we have only an unfocused and partial picture of what it is like.

Revelation 21: 22 gives us a fairly complete picture. John says he saw a new heaven and new earth, for the first had passed away. The new city had 12 gates of precious jewels and the description goes on, but note what is not there. There is no vandalism, no theft, and no graffiti. There is no one hungry, and no one is homeless. There is no ghetto in the kingdom. There is no illness or disease. There is no exploitation and there is no darkness, therefore no deception and exploitation, and everything is straightforward and above reproach. This snapshot is enough to give us clear direction. Our work and mission is to help bring this picture of the kingdom of God into reality.

Modern day Black Christians tend to see the kingdom of God as something so very different from our present reality that it is unattainable until it drops from the sky. We fail to see ourselves involved in that process, where

The Vow We Make

the first earthly order is passing away and the new one is coming into being. We are looking for something cataclysmic. Therefore, even the process of advocacy for our own people can be put off for the time when "Jesus comes back." However, Jesus tells us the kingdom of God is like a mustard seed that grows. As we involve ourselves in the liberation struggle, which now mandates socioeconomic struggle, we work to gradually make the kingdom of this world the kingdom of our God.

One example will suffice. Slavery as an economic system no longer exists. It once was accepted, welcomed without critique. Thank God, it has passed away. Today, the few examples of slavery that occasionally surface produce moral outrage. The world economy no longer accepts slavery as valid. Opposition to slavery did not drop from heaven but gradually came about. Our ancestors were part of that body of believers who worked to help make it so. They saw it as part of their mission and purpose. They left a charge for us to continue to oppose slavery.

Jim Mulholland in his book *Praying Like Jesus* makes the point that when we pray "thy kingdom come," we are making a vow. "We are pledging our willingness to allow God's kingdom to be established in and through us."[29] It is a vow to participate in the work to help the kingdom of God come "on earth as it is in heaven". Our ancestors responded and kept this vow as best they could. They have left the same charge to us. We must keep this vow and involve ourselves in kingdom work.

A CHALLENGE TO THE BLACK CHURCH

Our work on behalf of God's kingdom is a work in progress that moves us toward a different world than what we know now. Our charge to keep is divinely commissioned, historically indebted, and collectively attainable. On Sundays we vow to continue this challenging way of life when we collectively pray "Thy kingdom come, they will be done on earth as it is in heaven" and when we sing the old hymn's last verse:

> *Help me to watch and pray,*
> *And on Thyself rely.*
> *By faith assured I will obey,*
> *For I shall never die.*

EPILOGUE

Walk Worthy of Your Calling

A final word in summary returns to a scripture referred to earlier.

I, therefore, the prisoner of the Lord, beg you to lead a life worthy of the calling to which you have been called, with all humility and gentleness, with patience, bearing with one another in love, making every effort to maintain the unity of the Spirit in the bond of peace. There is one body and one Spirit, just as you were called to the one hope of your calling, one Lord, one faith, one baptism, one God and Father of all, who is above all and through all and in all.

But each of us was given grace according to the measure of Christ's gift...The gifts that he gave were that some would be apostles, some prophets, some evangelists, some pastors and teachers to equip the saints for the work of the ministry, for building up the body of Christ until all of us come to the unity of the faith and of the knowledge of the Son of God, to maturity, to the measure of the full stature of Christ. We must no longer be children, tossed to and fro and

*blown about by every wind of doctrine, by
people's trickery by their craftiness in deceitful scheming. But speaking the truth in love,
we must grow up in every way into Him who
is the head, into Christ.*

Ephesians 4: 1-7, 11-15.

I have long been fascinated by Paul's heartfelt and perhaps final request from prison to urge the church to walk
worthy of its calling. It is a challenge that requires an ex-
panded view of ministry and ideas. It is a call to mature
faith that cannot be shaken or deceived by the cultural context or the schemes of men.

I have offered these essays with the humility that Paul
speaks of, with the hope that the ideas presented will help
us in the maturing of our faith. I hope these essays will
begin an engaging dialogue among Black people of faith.
Throughout this book, I have attempted to raise our attention to the critical areas of Black Christian thought that we
must examine if we are to be a vibrant and relevant entity.

I have written not as an outside observer but as one
unashamedly Christian, unapologetically Black, and actively involved in the church. I love the Lord, the Black
Church, and Black people, so my critical evaluation at times
is uncomfortable and troubling even to me. Yet without this
kind of engagement, we will find ourselves on the ash heap
of irrelevancy and, more importantly, unable to fulfill the
mandate of our mission as the people of God.

I am firmly convinced that God's specific mission for us is to be a catalyst for Blacks on the North American continent. Though others meant it for evil, we find ourselves positioned in this moment of history as advocates for others in the African Diaspora and the mother continent. To go forward, our theology must be relevant to our situation, prayerfully critical in analysis, and cognizant of God's hand in our midst. The way we think and talk about God will determine whether we will be able to enjoy the bounty of his blessings and lead healthy, secure, and productive lives.

Let us not ignore the tone of urgency in Paul's letter. It is not a mere request to the church but a plea filled with a divine imperative. It is not to say that the church in Paul's day had not begun to mature, but it urges the church to push ahead for a change in ideas and approach to ministry.

Likewise, there is a divine imperative that is upon Black Christians. It involves accountability, risk, and a firmer grasp of reality than we have ever had before. Our people are in crisis, and if we love them and the Lord, we must do the hard work of evaluation, challenge, and change. I am not saying that there is no growth or no response to the needs of our people through new and appropriate ministries. Quite the contrary, across the country collective action is taking place in response to these critical needs. Let me give a few examples.

In 1993 concerns were raised by pastors and church members in Prince George's County and the metropolitan District of Columbia area regarding inequitable access to services provided by local banks and businesses. Churches were faced with severe challenges due to red–lining and other questionable practices. As a result, a group of pastors met to discuss means by which to gain economic empowerment and justice in their business dealings. After several meetings, the group decided to consolidate its efforts under the name Collective Banking Group. The Rev. Jonathan Weaver, pastor of Greater Mt. Nebo AME Church, was elected President and continues to serve in that capacity today.

Since its inception, the CBG has continuously grown to its present membership of over 150 churches representing over 200,000 persons. Today, the CBG member churches have been approved for more than $95 million dollars in loans, have on deposit in excess of $130 million dollars with area banking partners, and have offered numerous savings to the community–at-large in over 20 different areas of business.

In Houston, Texas, in 1989 a group of investors, which included two churches, formed the Unity National Bank. This is their vision and mission statement as recorded on their website.[30]

Vision Statement:
To be the financial institution that partners with Houston's underserved communities to create opportunities.

Mission Statement:
To build relationships with the organizations and citizens of underserved communities and provide convenient financial products and services.

They remain the only African American–owned bank in the state of Texas, with assets of over 56 million dollars. The efforts of the Ten Point Coalition in Boston have been well publicized. The Coalition was formed in 1992 by clergy in response to a gang shooting and stabbing at a funeral in the Morning Star Baptist Church. Less well known is the Harvard Study that documents that under the leadership of three key leaders—Rev. Eugene Rivers (founder of Azusa Christian Community Church), Rev. Jeffery Brown (pastor, Union Baptist Church), and Rev. Ray Hammond (pastor, Bethel AME Church)—the coalition was enormously effective in aiding the reduction of youth homicides at a greater rate than anywhere else in the country. Subsequently, a national foundation was formed, and Black clergy in other cities are instituting similar ministries.

It is not simply large churches or ministries that are caught with prophetic fire. The collaborative effort of Black churches may also be seen in Los Angeles, under the auspices of LA Metro Churches. In 1994, LA Metro Churches (LAM), a network of small to midsize African American churches, was founded to address growing hopelessness, joblessness, illiteracy, and high rates of incarceration among young African American men. In 1998, LAM successfully fought for major prison reform legislation, which mandates that ex-offenders work toward a GED as a condition of probation. LAM works in Los Angeles County to build the capacity of churches to meet the needs of their communities. Key leaders are Rev. Eugene Williams III (founder and executive director), Rev. Richard Boyd (pastor, Christian Unity Center), Rev. Winifred Bell (pastor, Mt Olive Second Missionary Baptist Church), and Rev. Al Cooke (pastor, Fort Missions, Fruit of the Holy Spirit Baptist Church).

The most hopeful sign of change and collaboration is taking place among Black Baptist denominations. In January, 2005, for the first time in 100 years, the leaders and delegates of the four major Baptists conventions will meet together in Tennessee to craft a common–ground agenda designed to address the critical social, political, and economic needs of the Black community. They will be led by Dr. William J. Shaw (president, National Baptist Convention, USA), Dr. Stephen Thurston (president, National Baptist Convention of America), Dr. Major L. Jemison (president, Progressive National Baptist Convention), and Dr. Melvin Von Wade, Sr. (president, National Missionary Baptist Convention of America).

These are but a few examples of the prophetic response to the Gospel challenge, but there is much more to be done. There is more than enough to do, and everyone does not have to do the same thing. As the writer of Ephesians says, there are many gifts given for the up–building and maturing of the Church. We must use our gifts collectively, in small and large ways. We all need a starting point. Rather than leaving this open–ended, but at the risk of seeming too elementary, let me give some examples of ways in which you can get started:

1. Form a study group to study the texts and essays presented here. Six to twelve people are more than enough to start the process. It is not important to agree with this text or author, but it is important to discuss the issues. Pastors, place this before your people, or if you are a lay person, place this book before your pastors and other leadership.

2. Begin a reading club. Transformation comes by the renewing of our minds. Two books are must reading: *Black Labor, White Wealth* and *PowerNomics*. Learn more about where Black people are in the world and our history before the Diaspora, where we were scattered, and what we have accomplished since then.

3. Evaluate the mission's ministry in your church. Is it focused simply from year to year on the emotional pull for the moment? Is it focused enough for long–term impact? Is it empowering those affected? Are there other groups with whom you can partner? Partner first. Initiate alone only as a last resort in order to be good stewards of the resources you have been given.

4. If your church has a school, push for an Afro-centric Christian curriculum there and also in your Sunday school.

5. Make informed and conscious consumer decisions when you purchase. Make a personal decision to make

your dollar "bounce" in support of Black businesses. Dr. Kenneth Whalum, Jr., pastor of the New Olive Baptist Church in Memphis, Tennessee, has what they call Bust – A Move –Monday (BAMM). Every Monday a busload of church members chooses a Black business to support, and they buy out as much of its inventory as possible.

6. Aggregate as much as possible. The collective is much stronger than the individual—politically, socially, financially, and spiritually. Think of ways to partner with others for empowerment.

7. Change inappropriate thinking. For example, we are all on the same skin–color team. Often Africans or Afro-Caribbeans have been taught to look down on African Americans and sometimes vice versa. Let's not play that game. It is a Willie Lynch game that has worked to keep the team effectively neutralized and the owner in power. In gambling the only sure winner is the owner of the casino. United we can own, control, and make a difference.

8. Begin a discussion group in your church that moves beyond the simplistic answers and wrestles with the relevancy of the Gospel. Most of all, prayerfully make the changes that are necessary so that you as an individual, and your church collectively, is a vital, vibrant witness of our faith in a living God. We have been left a blood–bought legacy and a Gospel challenge to bring Good News to the poor, release to the captives, recovery of sight to the blind, freedom to the oppressed, and to proclaim in word and deed the acceptable year of the Lord.

REFERENCES

1. Gayrud Wilmore and James H. Cone, *Black Theology A Documentary History*, 1966-1979 (Orbis Books: Maryknoll, NY 1979), p. 3.

2. Words by Charles Wesley (1707-1788). The most common tune is by Lowell Mason.

3. Claud Anderson, *PowerNomics The National Plan to Empower Black America* (PowerNomics Corporation of America: Bethesda, MD 2001), p. 6.

4. Ira Berlin, Marc Favreau, Steve F. Miller, editors *Remembering Slavery* (The New Press: New York, 1998), p. 205.

5. Jerome C. Ross, *Holy Bible* African American Jubilee Edition, "Jubilee in Leviticus 17-26" (American Bible Society: New York, 1999), p. 72.

6. Ibid.

7. Claud Anderson, *Black Labor, White Wealth* (Duncan & Duncan, Inc.: Edgewood, MD 1994), p. 157.

8. Ibid.

9. R. Alan Culpepper, *New Interpreter's Bible*, Vol. 9 (Abingdon Press: Nashville, 1995), p. 135.

10. Norman Kelley, "Rhythm Nation: The Political Economy of Black Music," Black Renaissance/Renaissance Noire, Summer, 1999, volume 2, number 2 from Rap coalition website.

11. Ellis Cose, *Rage of the Privileged Class* (Harper Collins: New York, 1995), p. 49.

12. Cornell West, *Race Matters* (Beacon Press: Boston, 1993), p. 38.

13. Ibid.

14. Deidre Mullane, *Words to Make My Dear Children Live*, (Anchor Books Doubleday: New York, 1995), p. 118.

15. Gayraud S. Wilmore, *Last Things First* (Westminister Press: Philadelphia, 1982), p. 11.

16. Eugene Genovese, *Roll Jordan Roll The World the Slaves Made* (Vintage: New York, 1976), p. 251.

17. op.cit. Anderson, *PowerNomics*, p. 5.

18. op.cit. West, p. 52.

19. Claud Anderson, *Dirty Little Secrets* (Powernomics Publishing: Bethesda, MD 2000), p. 190.

20. John McWhorter, The Washington Post, *"Diversity's No Longer the Point, Is It?"*, December 8, 2002; page B4.

21. Ibid.

22. See Carter G. Woodson, *The Miseducation of the Negro* (African American Images: Chicago, 2000), chapter VI.

23. J. Deotis Roberts, *The Prophethood of Black Believers* (Westminister: Louisville, KY 1994), p. 34.

24. Ibid, pp. 34-35.

25. James Mellon, ed., *Bullwhip Days, The Slaves Remember* (Avon Books: New York, 1988), p. 180.

26. op.cit. Cone, p. 15.

27. op.cit. Anderson, *Black Labor*, p. 68.

28. Ibid, p. 132.

29. James Mulholland, *Praying Like Jesus* (Harper: San Francisco, 2001), p. 53.

30. www.unitybanktexas.com

SUGGESTED READINGS:

Anderson, Claud. *Black Labor, White Wealth.* Duncan & Duncan: Edgewood, MD, 1994.

_____. *Dirty Little Secrets.* PowerNomics Publishing: Bethesda, MD, 2000.

_____. *Powernomics: The National Plan to Empower Black America.* PowerNomics Corp. of America: Bethesda, MD, 2001.

Berlin, Ira, Marc Favreau, and Steve F. Miller, eds. *Remembering Slavery.* The New Press: New York, 1998.

Cose, Ellis. *Rage of the Privileged Class.* Harper Collins: New York, 1995.

Felder, Cain Hope. *Troubling Biblical Waters.* Orbis: Maryknoll, 1990.

Genovese, Eugene. *Roll Jordan Roll: The World the Slaves Made.* Vintage: New York, 1976.

Hacker, Andrew. *Two Nations: Black and White Separate, Hostile and Unequal.* Ballentine: New York, 1995.

Kunjufu, Jawanza. *Hip-Hop vs. MAAT: A Psycho/Social Analysis of Values.* African American Images: Chicago, 1992.

_____. *Solutions for Black America.* African American Images: Chicago, 2004.

Mellon, James, ed. *Bullwhip Days, The Slaves Remember.* Avon Books: New York, 1988.

Mulholland, James. *Praying Like Jesus.* Harper Collins: San Francisco, 2001.

Robert, J. Deotis. *The Prophethood of Black Believers: An African American Political Theology for Ministry.* Westminster/John Knox Press: Louisville, KY, 1994.

West, Cornell. *Race Matters.* Beacon Press: Boston.

Wilmore, Gayraud S. *Last Things First.* Westminster Press: Philadelphia, 1982.

Wilmore, Gayrud S. and James H. Cone. *Black Theology: A Documentary History,* 1966-1979. Orbis Books: Maryknoll, NY, 1979.

Woodson, Carter G. *The Miseducation of the Negro.* African American Images: Chicago, IL, 2000.

DISCUSSION QUESTIONS

IS THERE A BALM IN GILEAD?

1. How did you interpret the opening text prior to reading this chapter?
2. Do you agree or disagree with the author's assessment of Black America? Why or why not?
3. Do you agree or disagree with the author's remarks on the Black Church? Why or why not?
4. What are your reactions to the author's conclusion?

AN AWESOME DECLARATION

1. What would you say has been the main emphasis of the Gospel?
2. When reading Luke 4: 18-19, what is your initial interpretation?
3. Do you agree or disagree that this text is over-spiritualized?
4. How are you and your community of faith working to fulfill the Jubilee declaration?

THE STRANGE AND UNUSUAL GOOD NEWS

1. What is your concept of sin?
2. What do you think of the author's assertion of sin in the text?
3. In what ways do you participate in collective action to meet human needs?
4. In what ways does your church participate in collective action with other institutions to meet human needs?

5. What is your assessment of the effectiveness in ministry of your denomination?

FROM DELUSION TO SANITY

1. What to you is most provocative in this essay?
2. Do you agree or disagree with the author's assessment of the "fearful Black man"?
3. Do you agree or disagree that there is a problem of Black self-hatred?
4. Has your church addressed the issue of single parenthood in the Black community and the lack of child support?
5. Do you agree or disagree with the author's assessment of leadership accountability?
6. Does the Black Church have a legitimate message to our community that only we can deliver, and what is that message?

WHERE IS THE FIRE?

1. What image comes to mind from the word "fire"?
2. What makes you outraged and why?
3. Do you believe God becomes outraged? Why or why not?
4. Do you believe that there should be "prophetic rage" in the church and if so, in what instances, and if not, why not?

FOR SUCH A TIME AS THIS

1. Do you disagree or agree with the challenge of the author?

2. What do you see as the top three challenges of leadership in the church?
3. What do you think the author means by an "active walk with God"?

NO CHEAP GRACE

1. What has been the emphasis on John the Baptist and his message in your church?
2. How is your church acting in proactive ways to realize the Gospel message?
3. What is your understanding of forgiveness and repentance, and do you agree or disagree with the author's interpretations?
4. Is "cheap grace" a reality that you believe we must be concerned about?

FROM EVIL INTENTIONS TO THE GOODNESS OF GOD

1. What role does Black history play in your church?
2. What do you know about the African Diaspora?
3. How do you understand God's will in the era of slavery?
4. What do you thing of Joseph's theology?

THE VOW WE MAKE

1. How often is the Lord's Prayer used in your church?
2. What do you see as the consequences for making a vow to God?
3. In what ways do we act to keep this vow or break the vow?